Best Wishes

Dave Swendsen

BADGE IN THE WILDERNESS

Badge
in the
Wilderness

My 30 Dangerous Years
Combating Wildlife Violators

David H. Swendsen

Stackpole Books

Published by
STACKPOLE BOOKS
Cameron and Kelker Streets
P. O. Box 1831
Harrisburg, PA 17105

The events in this book are true. The names of the people I apprehended or arrested have been changed. The names of the wildlife officers are real.—*D.H.S.*

Printed in the U.S.A.

Library of Congress Cataloging in Publication Data

Swendsen, David H.
    Badge in the wilderness.

    1. Swendsen, David H. 2. Game wardens—United States—
Biography. I. Title.
SH354.S94A33 1985   363.2'8' [B]   85-2783
ISBN 0-8117-1877-8

To all the state and federal wildlife officers who have carried a badge in the wilderness: men and women who have dedicated their lives to the protection of those cherished things that make up the wild outdoors; enforcement officers with whom I have watched Canada geese, listened to barred owls and whippoorwills, and drunk black coffee at 3 A.M.; and those wildlife officers I have missed along the trail.

Contents

Part I

ROOKIE DAYS

Part II
SEVERAL YEARS INTO THE FRAY

Part III
A NEW START, A NEW CHALLENGE

Contents 9

Part IV
THE WILDLIFE OUTLAW

Part V
THE WILDLIFE OFFICER

ACKNOWLEDGMENTS

I'd like to take just a few paragraphs to tell you about some of the people who caused this book to be written, some in their actual assistance, some in spirit.

First, I give humble thanks to a quiet, hard-working man who gave me life. Without his love and respect for wild places and living things, neither I, nor the words you read now, could exist. He taught me at an early age how a person can fall in love with a trout stream or a secluded piece of pheasant marsh. (The smell of gun oil and fly dope, as our trips were planned and gear readied, still linger for me in the air today.) From his example, I learned that wildlife limits are sacred, not to be twisted or bent to suit the occasion.

It's easy to be honest in the outdoors when there is no opportunity or enticement to be otherwise. By watching this sincere man wade up the stream of life, I learned that a certain pride and calm comes to those who set their outdoor code of conduct high and maintain that standard despite the outside pressures and popular incentives.

I will always be in debt to this man. I will always fondly remember my dad, now in his 80s, wearing his old mosquito-lotioned hat, casting carefully up into that big, trout-filled pool that he taught me is always just around the bend.

I want to thank Larry Jahn and Dick McCabe of the Wildlife Management Institute for their help and continued encouragement in the long, painstaking process of completing this book.

I must credit my friend Gerri Herrick for getting me back on track during the writing of this book, constantly correcting my writing blunders, doing much of the typing and re-typing, and giving me support and confidence to go on. Her love of wildlife and our mutual interest in Thoreau's writings caused our paths to cross.

Without Bob and Myke, Rollie, Lou, and Bryant, this book could not have been written. Only they know the important part each played in its creation.

But most important, I thank my Jacqueline for her support in the writing of this book. Her patience and unending understanding and strength, through the many years of turmoil and pain, made going on possible. She raised the children, often alone. She tagged the beaver. She sold licenses and permits. She answered the telephone. She took the complaints and the abuse. But she cried when I cried, laughed when I laughed, supported me when I was weak, understanding my foolish ways and dreams, my battles, my goals, and my many, many crazy adventures. She shared all my disappointments and frustrations, but was seldom able to share in the few victories. Through almost unending illness and pain, she has always been there to listen and hold my hand. Yes, you will find my wife always present between the lines on each page of this book; always helping, forgiving, encouraging, and loving; lifting me up to go on in my job and in my life, and to eventually put these words into print, a task far beyond my imagination.

INTRODUCTION

I have always been intrigued by wild animals and wild outdoor places. After carrying the badge of a wildlife officer for over a quarter of a century, I have come to believe that most people are curious about whales and wolves and mountaintops.

I have found, through the years, that my daily enforcement adventures always fascinated the people around me. As a Wisconsin conservation warden, I soon found that the public wanted to hear about the two local deer hunters who were caught hauling an illegal doe out of the woods. Expecting wardens to search the back of the truck, the hunters hid the doe under coats around the gearshift. Blood dripping through a hole in the floorboards created a trail that even a rookie warden could follow.

Later, as an agent for the U.S. Fish and Wildlife Service, I found that New Englanders were also interested, as was the judge, in the story of the New Hampshire hunter's claim that he shot an out-of-season moose in the rear end in self-defense. And then, as my wildlife law-enforcement duties shifted more to a supervisory role with the government, I found that people still wanted to hear about agent in-

Dave Swendsen accompanied New Hampshire Conservation Officers to investigate report of moose shot illegally. Top view shows what officers found: brushpile with moose's nose barely showing. Other view shows officers skinning moose before they carried meat down mountain. Deer hunter claimed that the moose, shot in the rear, had charged him and that he'd shot in self-defense.

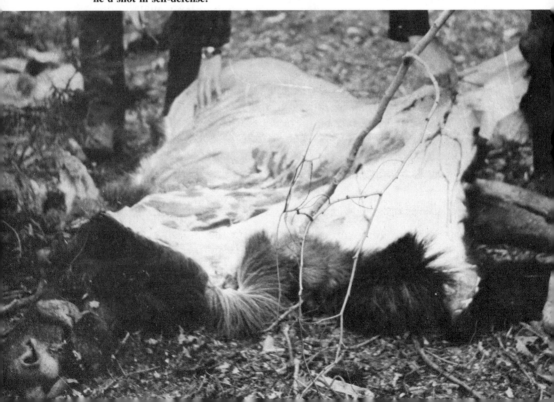

vestigations and such escapades as the trailing of illegal fur dealers and commercial fish and game outlaws through the downtown streets of Philadelphia, Boston, or New York City.

A number of years ago, I decided I would begin putting together what I felt were the most exciting and unusual game warden stories into book form. *Badge in the Wilderness* is the result of that beginning.

I had read many second-hand wildlife officer stories, written by various professional writers. It just seemed to me that such adventures were best told by someone who had climbed the mountain himself, waded the icy stream, or had lain shivering in the swamp—someone who had worn the boots of a wildlife officer, someone who had *been* there. This book is my attempt to take *you* there. The events are true. The names of the people I apprehended or arrested have been changed. The names of the wildlife officers are real.

When I was a boy, I read about the awesome wilderness and its frightening wild creatures. I read about how the pioneers fought an everyday battle with nature just to survive. Man needed to protect himself then from the unknown wilderness. I suspect we are now becoming the victims of those early battles we won with nature. After more than a quarter of a century battling the wildlife violator, I am convinced that our wildlife and our wilderness places now need protection even more than the pioneer did, protection from ourselves.

Little is known about wildlife officers. In the following pages, I hope to make you better acquainted with wildlife officers, especially some of those I have known. I have found them a special breed.

Some people have put labels on hunters and fishermen, labels like *slobs* and *white knights*. Maybe after traveling through the pages of this book, you will feel as I do about such labels.

But let's step back in time. Come back with me to a time when the words *game warden* or *wildlife officer* or *special agent of the U.S. Fish and Wildlife Service* meant little to me. A time when I was fascinated with all wildlife and the great outdoors.

PART I

ROOKIE DAYS

The end of a trout stream

I can still remember when I was not a wildlife officer. I especially remember an August morning in 1954.

It was just a week after my discharge from the Air Force. After taking off the uniform, I had hurried home to family, friends, and plans for a job and a future. I also hurried out to do some anticipated Spring Creek trout fishing. For the last three or four years I had dreamed a lot about the ravenous brown trout of Spring Creek. I often fell asleep at night picturing myself fishing and re-fishing those same dark, trout-filled holes.

So early that morning I said, I'm going trout fishing, and headed my old Plymouth for my favorite stream. My excitement had been growing with each turn in the road. I looked eagerly for the wooden bridge as I rounded the last turn in the road. Then my heart almost stopped beating. The interesting old bridge was gone. Instead, a high, concrete and steel bridge and a divided highway had taken its place. I hurried out of my car, carrying my dad's old bamboo flyrod. I still couldn't believe what I saw.

I climbed the steep man-made bank of the highway and stood on the new, white concrete of the bridge. An ugly ditch below me ran brown, dirty-looking water from the gentle, nightcrawler-producing rain of the night before. The drivers of the cars and trucks that went by must have thought I looked pretty foolish standing in my patched hip boots, holding a flyrod, peering down into the muddy ditch below.

Could I be lost? Where was my much dreamed-of trout stream? Could this man-made trench be my winding trout stream? What had happened to the alder-covered bends? Where was the "bottomless" springhole and the big inviting pool that was protected by the sprawling oak? And what about the trout? Suddenly I began to feel uneasy. A growing disapproval began to well up inside my chest. Why would anyone want to replace this once beautiful little stream with this dirty, nameless ditch? I had a lot to learn in 1954.

I still couldn't believe what I saw. Maybe I was lost. I looked quickly up the ditch. Yes, there was the red barn. It now stood in a treeless field. The big oak, the alders, and the giant willow that once lay half submerged in the springhole were all gone. The springhole was gone too. This ugly ditch was once my secret trout stream. "Progress" had come to Spring Creek. In my several years' absence, my trout stream, in all its God-made splendor, had become a mud ditch, in all its man-made shame.

I still stood on the bridge, my flyrod dangling from my quivering fingertips. In just a few short moments, my mood had tumbled from excitement to disbelief, to sadness and frustration. There was suddenly a heaviness in my heart that August morning. I couldn't understand this feeling then. I felt like I had lost a friend, a home, even a loved one.

I know now what I lost that morning; I know how important that winding trout stream was to my existence and my sanity. I think I know now why I suddenly felt such panic. My tiny piece of wilderness, wedged in between the hustle of this life, and the simplicity I sometimes needed were now gone. I didn't understand then. Spring Creek was now gone from that Wisconsin valley. Maybe part of me went with it.

I stood on the bridge, not noticing the trucks and cars whiz by. I was thinking about how, as a high school sophomore, I had first found Spring Creek. A friend had confided in me.

"Biggest trout you've ever seen," he said, looking around in case someone might hear.

He said they were brown trout, my favorite. I always felt, even with my limited experience, that brown trout grew bigger than brooks or rainbows. And they were always wiser, leaving my pole and me vibrating as the big one almost always got away.

My friend told me to see the old farmer who owned the land through which Spring Creek ran. So one Saturday morning, I rode my bike into the old farmer's yard. He was bent over the engine of a run-down looking tractor. I told the gray-haired old man I liked to fish trout.

"I wonder if you'd let me fish the stream behind the barn." I also asked about the springhole my friend had said had to be the home of some whoppers.

"Go ahead and soak a worm if you want. There's trout in that stream alright." Then lowering his voice to a whisper, as if he were telling me the combination to his safety deposit box, he said, "That springhole ain't got no bottom. And if it has, it's got to be sixty feet deep. Nobody catches anything in it though. But there are trout in it as big as a fencepost. I know, 'cause I've seen 'em.''

I found the secret trout fishing I had been searching for, and it was only a bike ride from my own backyard.

I waded the meandering, riffled waters of Spring Creek for several hours that Saturday morning and outwitted or lost wiley brown trout in almost every hole among the luxuriant growths of what I soon learned were pickleweed and watercress. When I had ten trout I cleaned them at the water's edge, marveling at their size and firm, pink flesh. Mom would like these. She always liked freshly caught trout. Dad wouldn't let us bring any overbag into his house. It didn't even occur to me that I might take home over the limit.

I didn't have any luck right in the springhole, though. Over the years I discovered it was thirty-two feet deep, icy cold, and that it really did have some big whoppers in it. One day, years later, I landed a four-pound monster. It makes me excited, even today, when I think of it thrashing and leaping and finally landing on the sandy bank near the willow.

The trout fishing was marvelous, not only that first day at Spring Creek, but many days through high school, during college vacations, and right up to when I joined the Air Force. Spring Creek had become a part of me.

The old, hard-working, but not very wealthy farmer and I got to be friends. We used to sit and talk when the fish weren't biting very well. Blowing pipe smoke out of his nose, he'd tell me about the trout as big as fenceposts that *he* knew were in the "bottomless" springhole. The old man died about the time I enlisted. Remembering him now, I don't think he would prefer ditches to springholes.

As I walked soberly back to my car that morning in 1954, I knew I'd miss the place more than the trout. It was my first lesson in how important an "insignificant" piece of wilderness can be to a person's existence. I think I may have decided then what direction my life's path should go. At least I knew I had to do something about what some called "progress."

Green as the forest

"You can't put everyone in the same basket." Those were some of the first words of priceless instruction I heard from Bill Waggoner, my first warden supervisor during my first and uncertain days as a Wisconsin conservation warden. My on-the-job training began with those words, words I will never forget.

Bill was trying to tell me then about labels put on people, labels like *slobs* and *white knights*. But mostly he was trying to tell me to make my start as a warden by trying to understand people. His words really meant that no two people react the same to being surprised by a wildlife officer in the outdoors. I was about to begin learning the most important lesson any law-enforcement officer must learn: understanding what makes people tick. After high school, five years of college, and the Air Force, I was just about to begin my education. I felt about as ready to be a warden in the northwoods as you might feel when they swing the glass door shut on your helmet and prepare you to step over the side on your first deep-sea dive off the New Guinea coast. But I was young then.

Bill Waggoner was a quiet, thoughtful-looking man. He seldom raised his voice. His life was the outdoors and its protection. Now Bill sent me off to work and learn with wardens little Ed Sealander and big Ed Manthie. Little Ed stood six foot one and big Ed was six foot three, so naturally everyone called them little Ed and big Ed.

I arrived for my first training assignment with little Ed, a shiny new badge on my well pressed uniform shirt, a stiff new pair of boots on my uncalloused feet. On my belt I carried a new gun I hoped I would never have to point at a man.

Looking back now, I see I had three things in my favor: I was enthusiastic about my new job, I had been assigned to two of the best wardens on the force, and I was just smart enough to know I didn't know a damn thing about being a state conservation warden. (About the enthusiasm—I've long since found out that when you're young and inexperienced, as I was, enthusiasm is about *all* you have to offer.)

I had been a warden now for thirty-seven long days and nights, and was still so green I could almost blend in with the trees. Little Ed became my assigned wilderness and wildlife instructor, counselor, and constant slave driver. The town we worked out of had a reputation for being tough on conservation wardens.

Ed and I had been working long hours together, attempting to apprehend nighttime deer hunters and illegal daytime fishermen. Suddenly, Ed's worn-out, wardenized car decided it had had enough. Wilderness roads and non-roads are hard on wildlife officers' cars. In those days, we bought our own cars and were reimbursed by the state at a rate of six or seven cents per mile. Gas sold for about twenty-six cents per gallon.

Ed decided to drive to his home town in the northeastern part of the state, trade in his old car, and spend a few days with his parents.

"Check out the dams on the Chippewa River early Saturday morning for illegal fishing activities," Ed called to me as he drove off in his old car. I was on my own.

At 6 A.M., I was perched among the trees, high above the first big dam. My binoculars were trained on two suspects fishing far below me in the spillway of the dam. Four fishing rods—two each were legal—protruded from wooden rod holders at the edge of the river. One fisherman was rolled up in his sleeping bag. His partner sat watching the rods. During the next forty-five minutes, I observed both sleepy fishermen tend the rods. At 7 A.M., I wound my way down the steep bank, coming in behind them. They now stood casting out into the clear bubbling current.

"How's fishing this morning?" I asked, coming up to the short, slight, balding man who had just reeled in his dough-ball bait. "I'm a state conservation warden. I'd like to take a look at your fishing licenses."

Both men stood unmoving, their mouths open. Then they looked at each other. Finally, the big, bearded, Mafia-looking individual started to talk. He told of a long, exasperating all-night drive from Iowa to this river.

"We were waiting until the stores opened up over the hill, so we could buy our non-resident licenses."

I suggested it might have been best had they slept in until the stores opened, and then thrown their lines in the water.

"Better pick up your gear," I told the two unhappy fishermen, "and accompany me up the hill."

All Iowa fishermen, I found out later, love catfish. So when the little guy pulled up their stringer with a nice big eight-pound catfish on it, I could almost see tears in his eyes.

From there we drove into town to see the local justice of the peace.

I had the big burly guy ride with me along with the rods and the eight-pound catfish. The little guy followed in his car. I kept thinking these guys sure looked like Chicago hoods.

As I had been previously instructed by little Ed, if I apprehended anyone, I should take him straight to the justice of the peace and he would help me process the culprit. Being brand new, I had only witnessed this ordeal once before and felt uneasy about the whole affair.

We pulled up at the home of the justice of the peace at about 8 A.M. All the shades were down. The place looked deserted. I knocked and rang the bell several times. Dillinger and Capone waited in the cars. Finally a woman came out of the house next door.

"Justice Johnson has gone away for the weekend," she said firmly.

What now? I had two villains under custody and didn't know what to do with them. Panicky, I finally remembered that little Ed had talked about trying to use another justice of the peace who lived in the next town. I didn't remember his name. But off we went.

I headed to the local know-it-all gas-station operator who, believe it or not, helped me. (At the time, *warden* was almost a dirty word in that town, and may still be.) I finally located by phone the justice of the peace.

"I'll meet you," he said, "at the high school. We can hang a flag in one of the classrooms and try to process your two non-resident catfishermen."

After what seemed like hours of going here and there and back again, I finally got my two Alcatraz-bound culprits to the school. I asked them to "wait in the hall." I went in and conversed in whispers with the "judge."

"This is my first solo case," I told him, "and second time in a courtroom." He informed me nervously that he had never held court or been in court on either side of the bench before. At that point, we pooled our vast talents and courtroom experience and decided on a plan of action.

I went into the hall and read a hastily drawn-up complaint to the tired prisoners. I also explained to them their rights. I told them they could plead guilty or not guilty to fishing without a Wisconsin fishing license. I was surprised to see them nod sadly and say, "We understand." I thought at the time they showed a great deal of patience.

We strode into the judge's flag-draped classroom. The justice stammered out the charge and asked for a plea, clutching his statute book in his hot, sweaty hands. I stood before him with Dillinger and Capone. Both defendants pleaded guilty.

The judge responded in an almost questioning and apologetic tone,

"Twenty-five dollars and costs?" Out came the cash, then the receipts for His Honor's and my prearranged fine. Now relaxed a little, the judge proceeded to give the villains a short lecture on non-residents who fish without a license in his county.

Dillinger and Capone and I walked out to our cars together. I returned their rods, and feeling quite relieved, returned the catfish to the little guy. Then I told the two, who had looked like but never acted like villains, where they could purchase a license. I started to walk away.

"Just a moment," the big, bearded man said, "I'd like the name of your supervisor."

I thought, here it comes. I had hauled them all over the county for three hours and taken them before an inexperienced judge (oh, inexperienced me). I wrote down little Ed's name and address and our chief's name and address at the state capital.

"Now that this is over," said the bearded man, "I want to write to your superiors. I want to tell them," he paused, "what a gentleman you have been during this terribly embarrassing incident. You do have our names on record, but I would like to introduce myself and my colleague. I am Dr. Harold Fuller, professor of law. This is one of my former students from law school, George Abernathy, now of the firm Abernathy, Abernathy, and Fosdick."

Walking on water

Warden trainees are expected to stand up under stress, strain, wind and rain, long hours, and no sleep. Sleep becomes almost a dirty word. Relaxation is a cup of black coffee, and the only females you see are spawning walleyes and doe deer. It seems that no one can pronounce the words *time off*.

When I first reported for duty the chief warden told me, "I'm sending you north into the brush country to get your training. Drive north tomorrow, and your new supervisor will assign you to some wardens who will teach you the ropes."

Working for big Ed and little Ed was tough duty. They worked me night and day from dawn until dark and it seemed from dark until dawn. After two months I was dragging. I started to wonder if the "ropes" they were teaching me were long enough to hang the two of them.

I was lonely, just married in February. It was now almost August.

I hadn't seen much of my pretty wife for almost two months. She was 350 miles away at the state capital, working for the State Department of Agriculture.

One evening, big Ed and I were working a night deer-hunting complaint and were parked on an old tote road near nowhere. This nowhere was about a quarter mile from a fresh-cut clover field. The field was a deer hunter's dream. The night before, the farmer who owned the land had counted thirty-five deer on the field at dusk, each chomping clover, foraging out away from the deer flies of the forest. At midnight, the farmer counted three shots. Big Ed got a call the next morning. Ed had a good rapport with the local landowners.

When we arrived, we found blood and a dragtrail (trail left by dragging a deer) in the field ending at the road. It was dusk now. Ed walked down the road toward the field, his size fourteens hardly making a mark on the sandy road. I stayed at the car and spread out our local green-lined map, north pointed north, on the hood of Ed's brush-covered car. With the map, Ed and I could judge the location and pinpoint distant shots if we heard any while we sat on the hood of the car waiting for nighttime outlaw activity. We heard shots almost every night.

The Eds were trying to make a warden out of this green college kid just discharged from the Air Force. I didn't know then that I was working for two of the most honest, most professional and hard-working wardens I would ever know.

Big Ed told me then a basic law-enforcement officer's truth, one that will never change: "A conservation warden *must be firm but always fair.*"

I found both Eds to be diligent, courteous, and patient. I also found them extremely observant and accurate about everything. When you question a suspect, they told me, only the truth can be used but certain leading questions "could be helpful." Little Ed would ask a just-apprehended deer hunter, "Did you shoot that deer to sell, or did you kill it just to take home for your family?" Either answer admitted to the killing of the deer. One answer just sounded better.

Big Ed would say things like, "To be a good warden you have to stay awake all night by eating sandwiches and drinking black coffee, (cream ruins your stainless-steel thermos). You have to learn to walk noiselessly through dry twigs and the always-present crunchy leaves, paddle a canoe soundlessly along a still lake shore as you check for illegal set lines off piers, walk through soft sand without making footprints, run on snowshoes, and shut car doors without even a click. Never slam a car door!" (I haven't slammed one, even in downtown Boston, for twenty-nine years.)

Little Ed would say quietly, but emphatically, that it was important that I learn to drive at night, hot behind an outlaw's car, with my lights out at speeds up to seventy miles per hour. (He also scared the hell out of me the first time we did it together. I hung on to my seat like a wide-eyed kid on a roller coaster.)

Big Ed told me that if I was going to last in the warden business I'd have to learn to smile at the judge when he turned loose a known outlaw I had proven guilty in court for the fifth time; learn not to breathe when the sound would alert illegal hunters, maybe ten feet away, loading their car with a just-killed deer or bag of speared fish; learn to see at night with my light-gathering binoculars; find out how to take license numbers off dirty cars as they go by on dusty, bumpy roads; learn to absolutely identify which hunter shot at what in the dusk, after hours, when all hunters are dressed alike in camouflaged hunting coats and the same kind of cap; listen patiently to aggravated "sportsmen" and landowners when they are unhappy with wildlife that's causing damage or with the state conservation department's "unwarranted" $1 license increases; get used to low pay, long hours, few fringe benefits, and wives complaining because they don't understand why wardens work day and night, weekends, holidays, birthdays, and even on special anniversaries.

And if I could master all these warden skills, I should practice crawling noiselessly through mud, across sharp rocks and around poison ivy. I should learn to pop up unannounced from behind a pine tree (officers should never be *found* hiding behind pine trees), in untarnished, full uniform and say pleasantly to a man spearing fish, "Good evening. I'm a conservation warden. You, sir, are under arrest." Finally, should I possibly learn all these things, during my "free" time I should practice *walking on water*.

As I waited for big Ed to return, I was thinking about all the new skills I was expected to acquire in the next few months. I began to get angry. I thought, just who the hell do these guys think they are, anyway? I've been married only six months, and I've been up here in the north boondocks for almost two months chasing deer shiners and no-license fishermen and working twenty-five-hour days. I hadn't seen my new bride, it seemed, for years. When big Ed gets back, I told myself, I'm going to tell him he can take this job and. . . .

I looked up, and there stood Ed. He had suddenly popped up through the dry twigs and leaves from nowhere, *without making a sound*. He was smiling. He could sense my anxiety; he had read my mind.

"How would you like to take this weekend off and meet your wife

for a second honeymoon?'' he asked in his quiet manner. "Little Ed
and I arranged for Jackie to get a free ride halfway here. We reserved
a nice motel room for you two for two nights. If you're interested, you
can leave tomorrow and come back Monday morning. You won't get
much sleep tonight, but what do you say?''

"You can—you can bet your size fourteen boots I'm ready for a
second honeymoon, sleep or no sleep!''

I didn't think Ed knew then how close I'd come to telling him
what he could do with the job. But looking back now, I guess both
Eds knew I was close to the breaking point. As wildlife officers often
do, they get a feeling about people and they do something about it
pronto.

It was a nice weekend. I didn't get much sleep and I didn't eat
any sandwiches or drink black coffee to stay awake. I came back on
Monday ready to continue the job of learning to be a more professional
wildlife officer—a job I continued working at and learning during every
one of the thirty years I prowled the outdoors.

Judge's trout stream

As I drove slowly along the unfamiliar, snow-covered road, I couldn't
help thinking, you are quite the rookie, game warden Swendsen. You
don't know where you are, or even what county you are in. Now how
do you expect to outwit a sneaky fish or game violater today? He'd
have to just about walk right up to you and give up. And then he would
have to help you find your way out of the woods.

It was the dead of winter, early morning, and cold—maybe fifteen
degrees below. I had my young and equally inexperienced black Lab
riding shotgun in the back seat.

As I turned a sharp corner in the road, I saw a fresh car-track in
the new snow. It came in off a side road and after a few hundred
yards, the car pulled to the side of the road. I caught sight of a man-
track leaving the car. The car had then gone on its way.

I stopped and got out. The man-track led off into the woods. I
didn't know what was back there that was worth checking out, but my
curiosity was getting the better of me. Even if I didn't know where I
was, what I lacked in woods knowledge I tried to make up with enthusiasm.

I put the dog back into the car. He was too excited. I took my
binoculars and clicked the door shut so as not to announce my arrival.
After a few minutes of walking through four inches of snow, I came

to a long hill. The man-tracks continued on down the hill. I heard running water. Maybe a pre-season beaver trapper, I thought. A hidden stream ran quietly through the woods ahead.

I stopped at a distance and looked carefully with my binoculars up and down the stream. Then I saw him. First, just a movement off to my left in the stream. I moved carefully until I was only a few feet from the water, standing behind a large pine.

My man was downstream about seventy-five yards. He was wading upstream toward me. He had a minnow seine with two poles over one shoulder and a large canvas bag on a strap over the other. If this was a trout stream, it was illegal to seine minnows here. I didn't know. I was still lost.

The man, dressed in hip boots and dark clothes, continued to wade toward me. Surprisingly, he headed right to the bank where I stood. He didn't look up as he picked his way along the bottom of the stream.

He splashed right up to my tree, reached down and pulled up a submerged minnow bucket from the undercut bank at my feet. He laid the canvas bag on the bank in front of me and was about to lay down the seine and poles. I suspected it was time to announce my arrival. I looked in vain for a second person who might have manned the other end of the seine. I could see none, nor any tracks to indicate there was another seiner.

"Good morning. Nice day to be out on the stream, isn't it?"

My "friend" looked up, quite shocked, and replied, "Who are you? A beaver trapper?" I pulled out my credentials, watching the man's eyes.

"I'm a conservation warden. What do you have in the bag?"

He looked like a little boy caught with his hand in the cookie jar. He looked at the bag, which moved a little—something was alive and wriggling inside. The man looked at me again, and with about ten pounds of guilt in his eyes, handed me the bag. I dumped it out onto the snow. Twenty-seven of the nicest, fattest brook trout I'd ever seen flopped out of the bag. Some were still kicking.

"What's in the minnow bucket?"

With a look of resignation, my hip-booted friend swung the bucket over to me and flipped open the top.

"Sorry to say, a few more trout."

I looked into the clear water in the bucket and saw two nice 1½- to 2-pound trout swimming around as best they could. They were beauties. Big enough to make me or any other trout fisherman want them tugging on the end of our line.

I had learned in my short career that getting angry with a violator of the fish and game laws not only is wrong professionally, but it also makes an officer careless and inefficient. So, even though I felt a little miffed at trout seiners, I decided to stay cool with my trout-taking friend.

"Let me have your hand. I'll help you up out of the stream." As I pulled him to the bank, I said in a calm voice, "You are under arrest for taking trout out of season and in an illegal manner."

The trout seiner, a local man, paid a $200 fine in the county court and lost his hunting and fishing privileges for one year. In those days in the north country (or any country), that was a big fine. The judge, it so happened, was also a trout fisherman. This wasn't the trout seiner's day. Those beautiful red-finned brook trout were taken from the judge's favorite stretch of *his* favorite secret trout stream.

I never did find out how or if the trout seiner managed to handle both ends of the minnow seine. But if he did have a partner who got away, I suspect my little ride down that snow-covered road and the judge's stern sentence made an impression on would-be trout seiners in that country for at least the next few months.

Oh yes, I did find out which county I was in and my way back home. As years went by, I became a more experienced warden who learned never to admit to being lost—a bit confused in my directions for three or four hours—but *never* lost.

Northwoods justice

Arriving at my first station in the northwoods of Wisconsin, I was full of energy, enthusiasm, and new ideas. My courtroom experience and skills, on a scale from one to ten, hovered just above the one.

It wasn't long before my long hours started to pay off in the apprehension of people who were out there violating the fish and game laws. All of my early apprehensions of people fishing without licenses or with too many lines were handled quickly by the apprehended person, usually by posting a bond at the sheriff's office. That is, until I apprehended Tom Balto, local fur dealer, junk dealer, locker plant operator, grocer, and influential businessman.

I discovered Tom's illegal act by examining his required fur records. I found no record of out-of-season beaver I knew Tom had purchased. But I had witnesses and receipts to prove the sale had occurred.

Wisconsin had then, and still has, fairly good fur regulations. Without strict control of the fur trapper, this multimillion-dollar business soon gets out of hand. Without tough tagging and record-keeping regulations, all fur suddenly becomes untainted, untraceable—"clean" and "legal." As an example of the incentive for cheating in the fur business, the 1978–79 going rate in the markets was $50 to $60 for a fox, $200 to $300 for a bobcat, and sometimes between $500 and $1,000 for a "legal" wolf hide.

Tom Balto's fur transactions weren't much different from those of most other fur dealers in the north country: profitable and questionable. Having found Balto's fur records incomplete, I told him he was subject to arrest; but since he was a local businessman, I would ask him just to appear in municipal court next Monday at 9 A.M. Tom wasn't angry. He acted like he'd been there before.

That Monday, I arrived at the courtroom in full uniform. My tie was straight and my shoes were Air-Force shined. I stood up before the judge to read the complaint against Balto. (That was the proper procedure in that county.) Balto sat slouched in his chair beside me, his hat on his head and a short, unlit cigar protruding from his mouth.

I leaned down and said quietly, "Mr. Balto, please take off your hat and take the cigar out of your mouth, and stand up before the judge."

"Oh, that's all right, Tom. You just sit where you are," said the judge. (There were only three of us in the courtroom.) "This won't take long. I see where the warden here has you charged with failure to keep complete and accurate fur records, in violation of 29.135 Sec. 6m, of the Wisconsin Statutes. How do you plead to that, Tom?"

"Well, Rob, if I plead guilty, how much you gonna fine me?" asked Tom, without taking the cigar out of his mouth.

"Oh, probably around fifteen dollars and court costs of five dollars."

"In that case, I guess I better plead guilty. I can't afford to fight it for twenty dollars. But I don't have the cash on me, Rob. Can I get it to you later?"

"Sure, bring it in sometime this week and pay the clerk. He'll give you a receipt."

I had just received my first lesson in northwoods justice. I can think now of an appropriate admonition by Oliver Wendell Holmes: "This is a court of law, young man, not a court of justice."

I stood speechless, still at attention, and feeling much out of place in my tie and clean uniform. This episode should have occurred at one of the local bars or a coffee shop, not here in the municipal court. I thought then, as I do today, that a court of law is a place where formality and strict rules of conduct must predominate over all actions by everyone present, especially the judge.

I was not totally surprised. I had been prepared for my first court appearance in my new county by my supervisor. He had explained northwoods courts as soon as I arrived.

"Prepare your case as if you were going to take it to the Supreme Court," Bill had said, "and don't be upset when you lose. Justice in this county is northwoods justice. We haven't won a real fish and wildlife jury trial for five years. Judges and prosecuting attorneys in this county often get their jobs with the flip of a coin. The few attorneys that are in the county get together over a cup of Main Street coffee and match for the upcoming openings."

I had now experienced my first day in municipal court. Bill had told me what would happen and Big Ed and Little Ed had given me some good advice about how to handle it. I decided to follow their advice and do two things. First, I would stay cool.

"Will that be all, Your Honor?"

"That will be all," the judge replied.

Then I turned to Balto and thanked him for appearing as scheduled. I told him I had his fur record books in my car and would return them if he would walk out there with me. Second, I decided at that moment that I was going to change fish and wildlife justice in this county. Somehow, by working hard and by convincing the people and the judge of the value of the northwoods fish and game, I would change northwoods justice. I had a lot to learn about people, judges, and justice.

In the ensuing years, I found that Bill was right about a lot of things. I remember having coffee one morning with the four attorneys in that county after a fish and game trial. (They won.) And I watched as the attorneys matched to see who would be the county prosecuting attorney for the following year. The loser had to take the job.

I also watched as six-man juries were quickly selected from the street, to hear and then render "not guilty" verdicts. The juries would let habitual and chronic violators go free time and time again. They were made up of some of the same town "availables" each time.

But in the next eight years, along with the defeats and hard-to-accept injustices, there came some victories, even in jury trials. I could also see some real public support for my fish and wildlife law-enforcement efforts. And I knew down deep that *that* was what it was all about.

I put a gun in his ear

Wildlife officers consider certain violations of the wildlife laws more criminal than others. Crimes such as shooting or taking wildlife out of season; taking protected species such as eagles or songbirds; selling or commercializing in wild animals and their parts; or taking wildlife in an inhumane or unsportsmanlike manner are wildlife crimes that I feel fit into this more serious category. Selling migratory birds is a felony under the federal Migratory Bird Treaty Act. These are crimes against everyone's personal sense of wilderness.

"Shining" or "jacking" is an underhanded and extremely effective method of taking deer, rabbits, and other animals as well as game birds. Shining rates high on the list of serious wildlife crimes. A deliberate violator will throw a powerful beam of light, usually from a car spotlight, into the eyes of a startled deer as it grazes at the edge of the woods in a forest opening such as a fresh clover field. The light surprises and often hypnotizes the deer as it stands, as if paralyzed, staring into the blinding glare.

A rifle, sometimes outfitted with a night scope, is shoved quickly out the car window. There is one loud rifle crack and the deer is down in a matter of seconds. Some shiners will use silencers or shoot with the gun barrel still in the car to cut down on telltale noise. Some will use quieter, small-caliber rifles which will often wound deer rather than kill them. Many shined and shot deer run off into the woods to die. Shiners are usually in too much of a hurry to take a chance on going after the wounded deer.

Wildlife officers throughout the nation spend hundreds of thousands of cold, sleepless hours attempting to apprehend nighttime deer hunters. From late June until early December of my first year as a warden, I worked night deer hunters 158 nights, every night but 32. My wife would probably be the first to say that was too much. But in August of 1955, with the help of several other volunteer deputies, I apprehended, prosecuted, and convicted 11 deer shining outfits in 14 nights.

Let me tell you about the first apprehension and give you some front-line experience out there where things happen. Deer shiners (jackers, in the East) do serious harm to deer populations in all states.

It was the blackest night I could remember. I stopped my car. There was a shovel lying in the middle of the road. On my left, the lights were hitting a house trailer that had been converted into a deer-hunting shack. There was a roll-away bed half in and half out of the open door. Moving? At 11 P.M.? On a Sunday evening, in the middle of nowhere in northwestern Wisconsin? Someone was moving out all the furniture from the deer camp. But it was someone who hadn't confided in the owner.

Don Balzer, my game manager partner for the night, and I had been sitting out on a potential deer-shining field since dusk. We had had a long week.

"Don, let's head for home," I finally said. "We'll check out a few likely fields on the way."

We had just shined a field and had seen no deer. We started west on the Old Lampson Road when we noticed car lights approaching us from the west. I was suspicious because the lights seemed to suddenly appear just over the hill, instead of gradually lighting up the horizon and then becoming brighter as they got nearer.

As we met the car, I read a partial Minnesota plate number off the front. When I tried to get the rest of the plate number off the back—an old warden trick I was just learning—I observed a two-wheeled trailer loaded with what appeared to be white appliances. There was a Minnesota trailer license on the trailer, but I couldn't get the number. We had no legitimate reason to stop the car. We drove on about a half mile and there was the shovel lying in the middle of the road.

Suddenly it all fell together. The occupants of the Minnesota car were stealing all the furniture from the house trailer/deer-hunting camp when, right in the middle of the fun, some rookie game wardens appear out of the night.

Shutting off the engine, I stepped out of the car and found the August night just as silent as it was dark. But in the silence I heard someone running. Someone was escaping behind the house trailer, escaping into the woods. I heard two people running, one to the right and one to the left of me as I faced the trailer. Then I heard them stop.

"Looks like someone is moving out, Don," I said in a loud voice. "I'll just throw this shovel off the road and we'll be on our way." I went back to the car and whispered to Don, "Slam the car door two times, drive off, and come back in about twenty minutes."

Don slammed the door twice and drove off, leaving me standing in the middle of the sandy road, my big six-cell flashlight in my hand, my cuffs and a .38 Smith and Wesson on my belt, my binoculars around my neck, and my citation notebook and pen in my pocket. Even though I had been at my northwest Wisconsin station for less than a month, and a rookie Wisconsin warden for only three months, my training had been good. I didn't get out of the car at night without my "survival gear."

As soon as Don and my car disappeared down the road to the

west, I heard one of the runners start back towards me. The other one started moving again, still disappearing to my left.

I just stood in the road. It was dark as the inside of a bear's stomach. I couldn't see ten feet in front of me. I could hear someone shuffling closer and closer toward me. Now that someone was on the road about twenty feet from me, I figured I could outrun him if I had to. I switched on my big "dog house" gas-bulb flashlight and aimed it directly into the eyes of a short, slight, gimpy man.

"Hold it right where you are. I'm a conservation warden, deputy sheriff. You're under arrest." I moved quickly up to the man as he tried to shield his eyes from the bright light. "What are you doing out here at this time of night?" I asked.

"Just helping a friend move," he replied, starting to recover from the unexpected surprise of the light coming out of the darkness.

"Yes, but your friend doesn't know you're helping him move."

I put the short, not very dangerous-looking man up against a tree and searched him. I was taking down his name, Alden Monroe, when Don and my car reappeared from the west.

My patrol car was as new as I was. As yet, I had no two-way radio. I gave Don instructions to load up our number one thief and head for the all-night restaurant about ten miles down the road, where he could call the sheriff and get him on the scene.

I decided to stay near the trailer. I fully expected the Minnesota car to return to retrieve my prisoner Alden and our unknown runner thief. The second thief took off all the faster when I arrested Alden. Alden shouted, "You might as well come in too, Ward," or some name that sounded like Ward or Warren.

Again my car's taillights disappeared, this time to the east. Again, it turned very dark and very quiet. I could no longer hear our second culprit running through the woods, only the hoot of an owl saying "who—who—who—."

I found a sitable stump just off the road in the woods across from the house trailer. I sat down and lit my pipe. I was prepared to wait it out.

To my surprise, I didn't have long to wait. Thirty minutes after Don left, the horizon to the east started to grow lighter. I could hear a car moving on the road toward me. I checked my phosphorescent-dialed watch. It was now 12:30 A.M. Just before the lights bounced up over the hill at me, I knocked out the pipe and ground the ash into the damp moss with my heel. Yes, it was the same car, a 1955, light-colored Ford. It had a Minnesota plate, first numbers E45. It pulled up even with the house trailer and stopped.

I peered over the alders into the car. There were two men. They swung a spotlight over toward the trailer. Then they drove slowly beyond the trailer, hit their brakes, and began to turn around using the old bootlegger turnaround. (To do a bootlegger, you pull hard to the wrong side of the road, cramp your wheel hard right and back as if you're leaving the bank with all its cash, but no permission.)

I crouched as the car's lights swung over my head. The car rolled back up to the house trailer directly in front of me. The driver turned off the engine. The windows in the car were open. I assumed the occupants were listening for their two partners-in-crime. I figured they could almost hear me breathe; they couldn't, I didn't. Then I heard the passenger whistle out the window toward the deer-camp trailer.

The moment of decision was upon me. Law-enforcement officers, unlike many professionals, can't wait to ponder their next move. They have to act on the spot. I said to myself, if you want these characters, it's now or never.

I came bounding out of the ditch like a hurdler out of the blocks (I was a hurdler in high school). I was at the driver's window in four bounds. My blinding flashlight glared into the faces of the two astonished men.

"Conservation warden, you're under arrest."

The driver, the older of the two, reached toward the ignition with his left hand (the '55/'56 Fords had the ignition on the extreme left side of the dash). My .38 came out of its holster almost by itself, and I found myself nudging it firmly into the driver's neck.

"Hand me the keys and don't move a muscle," I heard myself saying. To my surprise, the driver and his frightened passenger followed my instructions like robots. "Now slide out, one at a time, and keep your hands out where I can see them."

The driver started to slide out the door toward me. I caught a sudden glimpse of something shiny on the seat between the two men.

"Hold it right there," I shouted, emphasizing my words by pressing my .38 directly into the driver's left ear. Keeping the gun barrel in that attention-getting position, I reached across the front of the driver with my flashlight hand and snatched a fully loaded .22 automatic pistol from the car seat. It was lying conveniently at the right hand of the car driver who was now sweating profusely. I jammed the .22 into my belt.

"Out! One at a time and up against the front of the car in the headlights." (Big Ed and Little Ed's recent instructions were still echoing in my ear.) "Spread your legs and lean into the car." Once they were spread-eagle, off balance, their faces looking into the car headlights, I started to search the two men.

"What are you two doing out here at this time of night?"

"Hunting deer," the driver said.

At first I was stunned, expecting an answer like "picking mushrooms" or "on our way to church" or some such logical smart retort. But with a feeling of having the best poker hand, I pressed on.

"What do you mean, hunting deer?"

The driver, who said his name was Harold Kringle, told me how he and his son, the other passenger, had just come from hunting deer with the light and the gun that were lying on the back seat. After searching Harold and his son, I cuffed them together and had them sit on the hood of their car, in the headlights. I went to search the car.

Sure enough, there was a plug-in spotlight and a loaded 30-30 caliber deer rifle in the back seat of the car. In the trunk I found a tarp with fresh blood and deer hair all over it. A big hunting knife coated with dry blood and hair also lay in the trunk. It appeared that Harold had figured out that getting caught hunting deer with an artificial light wasn't as costly as being charged with breaking and entering and larceny. He was to find out that wasn't true.

I proceeded to take down all the personal information on Harold, who also possessed ID cards for Harry Cringle, Harvey Krencle, Henry Cringo and H. Krueger. His son was a big seventeen-year-old. I questioned both men about the trailer and appliances and bed halfway out of the deer-camp door. But I could see they had decided they would stick to their deer-hunting story, which, of course, was also true.

I could soon see the eastern skyline getting brighter. In a few minutes, the sheriff arrived with Alden, my first prisoner. Don pulled up in my car right behind the sheriff.

"Good morning, Jim," I said. "Sorry to get you out of bed."

"Thanks for calling," he replied.

Jim Scharhag, the sheriff, was big, honest, and professional. He and his wife had been patient with me during my rookie days and in a short time we became friends. Jim knew the woods and how those who lived in the backwoods schemed. He had grown up there too.

After passing on my information and handing over the two culprits to Jim, we closed the camp. Jim left with all three prisoners in his car; Don followed in Kringle's car. I stayed behind with my car. I said I was going to roam around the camp to see if I could track down Ward or Warren, or whatever his name was.

I wandered around in the heavy woods for about an hour, with no success. I kept calling, "Come in, Ward. Your friends are all under arrest. You might as well come in too." I lost his trail where he headed like a bull into a cedar swamp. I wasn't about to spend the rest of the night being eaten alive by mosquitoes even though he might.

Little did I know that the sheriff had better success. After leaving with the three prisoners and driving back to the main highway, Jim turned south toward town and the county jail. As he came over a slight rise, he saw something on his right disappear back into the woods. Jim, being a pretty sharp cookie, drove on down the road for several miles. He waited a few minutes for a northbound truck, then slipped in behind it and shut off his lights. When he got back to the spot where he had seen "the something" disappear into the woods, he wheeled off the road, aiming his bright headlights directly at the edge of the woods.

There stood Warren Grass, 6'5", 280 pounds, shirt torn off his black hairy chest, one shoe on, one shoe off, mosquito-bitten, sweating like a busy butcher and so tired and thirsty, his tongue hung out. He didn't even move.

The sheriff opened the door and said, "Get in, Warren." (He knew Warren from past exploits.) Warren climbed slowly into the car like a worn-out walrus.

Later that night, or I guess early that morning, we found the trailer with the stolen appliances. It was on an old road near Warren Grass's home.

Grass and Alden Monroe pleaded guilty in county court to attempting to steal a bed. They were given one year active probation. Kringle (we think his real name) pleaded guilty to hunting deer with an artificial light. (We never found the deer.) He was given the minimum fine of $100 and 10 days in the county jail. His gun, knife, and light were forfeited to the state. Kringle's son was not charged since he was a juvenile. Unfortunately, juveniles were then, and often still are, sent back by the courts with no restrictions. I have found that some juveniles soon become old enough and habitual enough in criminal behavior to be a real problem to themselves and society.

The carrying out of these sentences on Kringle, Grass, and Monroe is a story in itself and unfolds in a later chapter about judges and courts and the way justice is sometimes carried out strangely.

Unexpectedly, I was to check out, and arrest Kringle and Monroe several more times in the next eight northern Wisconsin warden years. Violating the law, especially fish and game laws, was a way of life for them. It was a way of life for many of the "live off the land, northern Wisconsin brush savages," as I used to call them.

There was a feeling of justified poaching felt by many of these people. Maybe this problem has a historic background, almost like that of the commoner taking game from the English king's rich, fenced-in lands. It's pretty hard to convince someone that his poaching is really a theft from his neighbor and eventually himself, not from the king, the state, or the local game warden. I suspect this local, "OK to steal wildlife from the state or federal government'' attitude, held by many users of the outdoors, can cause serious problems for wildlife populations and our nation's wilderness places.

My surprise appearance, just when Harold and Alden were in the middle of one of their little exploits, was almost uncanny. I never considered either man really dangerous or malicious, and I always treated them as big Ed insisted, fairly but firmly.

The fact that I repeatedly caught them in the act was not mysterious at all. This happened for two reasons: Harold and Alden were always out there violating the laws, and my philosophy was that ''wardens can't catch anyone staying at home by the fire.'' My wife would agree that I was usually *not* at home by the fire—to her patient disapproval and to Kringle and Monroe's continuing chagrin.

A warden's best friend

People who worked as my deputies, and especially those who helped at night, will appear and reappear throughout the pages of this book. Without deputies, wildlife officers couldn't really do their job. There are times when, without deputies, wardens might not survive.

Wildlife officers shouldn't work alone at night; many do. I worked many nights alone, but knew it wasn't right. Wildlife officers always try to work at night with another officer or to commandeer some conscientious deputy. I have always felt two officers can handle three, four, even a half dozen violators under most conditions, but an officer alone is not much better than one-on-one, at night.

I had some of the greatest help from other wildlife officers, game and fish managers, sheriffs, deputy sheriffs, policemen, forest rangers and forest managers, special part-time seasonal wardens, and occasionally just ordinary citizens that any wildlife officer could brag about. These deputies worked night after night, with no extra pay. In fact, many state employees often were criticized by their single-minded bosses for the extra time their employee put in with me to protect the resource. The deputies' help and cooperation could only come from the same dedication to the resource that most wardens feel inside. There was no other reason for these irreplaceable deputies to be out there, when they could be home by the fire.

One of my deputies was different from all the rest. He could run faster than any of the others. He could hear a car moving on a gravel road ten miles distant. He could swim faster and farther than anyone.

Portrait of Midnight, Swendsen's 105-pound black Labrador retriever that thought he was a person. In Midnight's role as warden patrol dog, he carried out many duties in ways that were the envy of human wardens. He was in on the arrests of a good many game-law violators.

He could smell fear in a man from twenty feet away. He never told any dumb jokes or spilled coffee on his lap or mine. He didn't growl or complain about being tired or cold or being ready to go home. In fact, he didn't talk at all. This deputy might have been classified as a warden's best friend.

This friend was my ninety-five-pound black Labrador. His name was Midnight. My neighbors often kidded me about sticking my head out the front door just before I went to bed and calling, "Midnight!" They always laughed and said, "We know it's midnight. You don't have to shout it all over the neighborhood every time you go to bed."

Midnight helped me make apprehensions when I would least expect it. Although untrained as a police dog, Midnight made many cases through the years, some of these you will read about in later chapters.

But Midnight's most dramatic deputy work took place at about 2 A.M. on a black morning in September. He was just about nine months old, still a pup. I took Mid along that night only because I couldn't find any human help.

"Why don't you take the black angus with you tonight?" my wife Jackie asked. "I don't want you to go alone. Besides, he'll keep you company. He'll be someone to talk to and he won't talk back."

Secretly, between you and me, I always expected Midnight, who thought he was a person anyway, to someday speak up and say something. He often looked up at me with those big brown eyes, cocked his head, and started to say something. Then he would appear to change his mind (it really wasn't worth the effort anyway).

So off we went into the night on a deer shining complaint. I had received the complaint from a farmer who lived across the lake from my home. Sure enough, by midnight (the *time*, not the dog), I had apprehended three young people attempting to kill a deer in that farmer's field. I had no help from Midnight. In fact, he was mostly in the way and wanted to lick the hand of one of the young, harmless, teenaged violators.

By 1:30 A.M., I had taken the gun handler to jail and his juvenile friends home. Midnight and I were now also headed home. My "helpful" deputy was sprawled out across the back seat, whimpering and sleep-running as he dreamt of bones or rabbits or pheasants, or whatever sleeping dogs dream about.

As I drove toward home on the main highway, I was surprised to see the taillights of a car disappearing over a little knoll just off to my right on a dead-end road. I knew the farmer who lived on that road. He owned only an old pickup truck. Besides, old man Johnston always went to bed with the chickens, and it was now long after midnight (both the time and my sleeping deputy).

I drove my car south on the highway, just out of sight of the dead-end road. Then I doused my headlights, threw my special back-up, taillight shut-off switch, and swung around back onto Johnston's road. When I rolled quietly up to Johnston's clover field, I saw the car.

I also saw a spotlight working over the field. The light appeared to be coming from the left front window. A gun barrel protruded like a cannon out the left rear window. The gun was aimed at a big buck deer that now stood staring, hypnotized by the glaring light. I stopped and waited, holding my breath, listening for the shot.

In my county court, you better have a *corpus delicti* if you expect to get a conviction. Well-meaning citizens often ask me why wardens don't stop serious law violators before they kill the deer or spear the fish. If wardens did that, no habitual violator would ever be found guilty in court. Besides, the loss of one deer or a bag of fish—if a conviction takes place—can save hundreds or thousands of deer or fish in the future.

Just then, the farmer's pickup truck started up and came out of the driveway. I appreciated Johnston's concern, but his arrival wasn't timely. I didn't need another helpless deputy. The light and the gun were quickly pulled into the car as the farmer's truck came slowly over the hill. I decided I'd better stop the car ahead of me now, or I'd have no case at all. If the deer shiners roared off and got rid of the gun, I was out of luck.

Before the farmer's truck arrived, I gave the sheriff a quick call on my car radio and told him where the action was. I then pulled up directly behind the shiner's car, threw on my lights, siren, and red light. With the red light flashing, I jumped out of my car and headed for the driver's side of the unmoving car ahead.

I saw no gun as I approached the front window. My deputy had jumped out too. (He went off to do what dogs usually to after being couped up in the back seat of an automobile for an hour or more.) I hoped at least this time he would stay out of my way. As I approached the driver's open window, I made one of the stupidest statements of my four-month career.

"Conservation warden, you're under arrest. Everyone out and alongside the car."

I suddenly realized my mistake as seven men piled out quickly and lined up alongside the car. They acted like they were being arrested by a team of wardens coming at them from all directions. Little did they know I was alone and quite incapable of controlling them if they decided to run off into the woods or jump me on the spot. I could tell these twenty-year-olds had been drinking. I could smell a strong odor of alcohol when I got near them.

I had fairly good control of the group, until they began to sense that I was the only warden there. I wanted desperately to search their car for the gun and the light I had seen earlier. But my crowd control started to break down once they saw no other badges or deputies. I couldn't leave my prisoners for a second.

My gun remained properly in its holster. Several of the men, now over the surprise of seeing my red light flash upon the night scene, started to become belligerent and move slowly toward me. I knew I still didn't have the evidence, the gun and the light. And so did they. Without the gun and the light I couldn't implicate them in a charge of shining deer while in possession of a firearm.

Just when I was about to lose control of the whole situation, the entire atmosphere changed. The men stopped moving toward me; instead they backed up and stood at attention against the car. Not a word came from their open mouths. I saw sudden fear in their eyes. Each young man stared down at my feet. Surprised, I looked down too.

Standing in a pointing position, the hair on the back of his huge neck standing straight in the air, his lips curled back exposing his long white teeth, was ninety-five-pound deputy Midnight. I had never seen him look so formidable. His timing was unbelievable. Truthfully, I was more surprised than the seven young men, who now stood stiffly at attention.

I grabbed my chance like a brown trout grabs a mayfly in June. I said sharply, "Midnight hold." I had never taught the black angus to guard prisoners, but I had taught him to "hold," when on point or preparing to crash into the brush after a pheasant or partridge. The big black dog reacted just like a well-trained Marine. Now his lip curled back another inch and a low continuous growl came from deep within his throat. Midnight had stood at "hold" for as long as twenty minutes during his hunting training and I knew he would now guard my prisoners while I quickly searched the vehicle for the gun and light.

I found the light still plugged into the cigarette lighter on the dash. A quick search under the seats and under the dash with my big flashlight revealed no gun. They must have thrown it when they piled out of the car. I walked around the back of the car and flashed my light along the road on the passenger side of the vehicle. The right rear window was open. Ten feet from the window a .22 automatic rifle stood, barrel down, in the soft sand of the road ditch. The gun must have hit the fence and bounced back: it looked like a flagpole announcing its location.

I picked up the gun carefully to protect any fingerprints I might take later from the weapon. For effect, I carried the gun and the light around the front of the violators' car, past the men and my still growling deputy. Now they knew I had the evidence I was looking for. I locked the light and gun in my trunk.

While my unmoving deputy continued to hold his prisoners, I took down all their names and addresses and the plate number off the front of their car. I found out with a few quick questions that after a National Guard meeting, while building a little false courage (with a number of tall beers) at a local bar, the young men decided to "go shoot a deer." Right now they were pretty sober and subdued.

I told the driver to follow me in his car to the sheriff's office about ten minutes down the road.

"Climb into my patrol car," I said to the rest of the culprits. "The sheriff is on his way here." None of the men moved.

"I'm not getting in that car with that monster," one of them answered.

No one wanted to get into my car with the big dog. Just then, with his car's red light flashing, the sheriff swung off the highway onto our road. All the men were put into Jim's car. My deputy climbed back into the back seat of my car and took up his former relaxed position, filling up the whole seat.

Once Jim and I had all the men locked in jail for the night, I told Jim about Midnight's guard tactics, curled lip, continuous growl and all. Jim liked dogs. He knew Midnight well.

"I can't understand Midnight's change of character from the friendly big guy with the wagging tail to the ferocious deputy out there on the road."

I told him my secret. Midnight had always detested the smell of alcohol. When he came upon the arrest scene and smelled these men, smelling strongly of beer, he suddenly became my awesome deputy even without a superman phone booth.

Looking back on that night, I can be thankful for Midnight's timely and dramatic arrival. It just proves that one green warden can arrest and maintain absolute respect and control over seven intoxicated, ready-to-become-violent violators—as long as he has one long-toothed, bristling, growling, ninety-five-pound deputy to get their attention.

Wardens in the movies

It wouldn't be fair to try to convince you that there's no fun or foolishness in being a wildlife officer. But me in the movies? How foolish can you get? Wildlife officers are called on to perform many unusual tasks. I'm sure that acting in the movies shouldn't be one of those tasks. It is not for me. Let me explain to you just why I will never be a Humphrey Bogart, or a Sergeant Preston of the Royal Canadian Mounted Police.

Somewhere, way back on the dust-covered shelves of the Wisconsin Department of Natural Resources (formerly the Wisconsin Conservation Department), there is an old film stored away. If you were to find this film, its title would read *Protectors of the Outdoors*. I made my start and finish in the acting business in that classic of the fifties. It wasn't meant to be a farce, but putting me in it almost made it one.

When the department's moviemakers came to the area headquarters in my town, I was commandeered by my supervisor to help get the movie made. I was going to be the prop man, location arranger, and line coach for the warden actors. Russ DeBrock, then warden in the adjoining county, had been selected for the opening scenes of the movie. Russ, now a warden supervisor in the northeastern part of the state, is a big, good-looking guy—a natural for the part.

I was told to help Russ with his lines. I was to do this while trying to locate an untrodden field of snow (in late March), a spotted fawn (they lose their spots by fall), a pair of snowshoes, a piece of rope, a small uninhabited shack, and a place where the camera crew could have a cup of coffee. All this for the introduction and opening scenes.

Next, we needed someone to play the part of the villain, who would be caught with an illegal fawn tied to his shack. Warden Cliff Freeman became the hard, cruel villain. Cliff, a former wrestler, was really a big softy, but looked the villain.

First we had to find a field. It was early spring and little snow was left in the north country. We went north eighty miles until we found our field. We had trouble finding a fawn with spots. Deer mate in the fall, have their fawns in April, May, or June. Here we are in late March, asked by some scriptwriter from southern California to come up with a spotted fawn in the snow.

But don't underestimate wildlife officers. We know that deer-farm deer often mate at odd times as confinement seems to cause some mix-up in the normal sex drives of the animals. We found a fawn that was born in late August and still had spots.

Wardens then always carried rope and snowshoes in their cars. Today, wardens ride snowmobiles to keep up with the motorized sportsmen of the day. I had the rope, but had just taken out my snow-shoes from my car. The snow was gone in my county. After some scurrying around, we found an old pair in Freeman's car. Now we waited for DeBrock to arrive. He was tied up in court.

The cameras were set up on the road, facing out toward the snow-covered field. The introductory scene called for a Wisconsin warden (DeBrock) to come out of the woods, snowshoe across the unblemished snow, and disappear into the woods again. This would take place as the narrator went through a short introduction to *Protectors of the Outdoors*. The next scene would show DeBrock (still on snowshoes) catching the villain at his shack. A deer would be tied to the porch. The script then called for an arrest of the villain and a dramatic seizure of the deer.

The cameras were ready. The director was ready. Villain Freeman was ready. The deer was ready. Bill Waggoner, my supervisor, was ready. I stood holding the rope, a fawn on the end of it. Waggoner

The movie camera was rolling when Swendsen, then a fairly new Wisconsin warden, put this spotted fawn on his shoulders and snowshoed across the scene. *Photo by Wisconsin Conservation Department (now DNR)*

looked at his watch and then at me. I could see the wheels turning in that punctual mind of his. He's thinking, Swendsen knows the lines and what's supposed to happen out there. He had to learn them to help DeBrock, who still hasn't and might never arrive. I could see Bill had made a decision. "Let's run through the opening scenes using warden Swendsen," he said to the director. "When DeBrock arrives we can run over it again and use the best of the two."

My dramatic movie career was about to begin. The cameras began to roll as I pulled on the snowshoes and, in full uniform, started toward the congregation of helpers and department employees grouped on the road. I could tell the shoes were pretty loose as Freeman wore size fourteen (or larger) shoes. I couldn't seem to cinch them up right.

Just as I approached the camera, full face, my left snowshoe came off. I went head over snowshoe. I didn't think it was very funny; but as I crawled up out of the snow, everyone on the road was doubled up laughing. They finally stopped the cameras. Once everyone stopped enjoying my humiliation, the director decided we could readjust the camera setup. I could go back into the woods. There was just enough unblemished snow to try again.

I made damn sure Freeman's snowshoes were on tight this time as I headed for the cameras again. Without any problems, I trudged by the lenses and swung toward the woods, confidently hurrying my pace (according to the script) in anticipation of catching the cringing villain at his shack. Just as I approached the trees, my right shoe caught on a large, submerged branch. I went crashing again on my face into the snow.

This time I had to laugh too. As I rolled over to look back at the road, I wished I had the camera. People were rolling on the ground. They were in hysterics. I looked in vain for DeBrock. He was safer in court. The cameras were still running.

The director, after rubbing his chin and wiping the tears from his eyes, decided he could probably splice things together. He would leave out my two swan dives and salvage this monumental introduction to *Protectors of the Outdoors.*

But my movie career wasn't over. We went into the woods and tied the spotted fawn to the shack. They placed villain Freeman cowering next to the deer. I was still on snowshoes. (No, I wasn't going to fall down again.) The snow had been brushed from me and I was now hooked up for sound with microphone and wire. The script had me come suddenly upon the fawn and the "frightened" 260-pound Freeman.

My lines were pretty simple. They were, "Just a minute, Swartz. Stay where you are, you're under arrest." (The script writer obviously didn't know any more about wardens' arrests than he did about spotted fawns and snow in late March.)

Cameras started to roll again. I strode into the scene without falling or stuttering.

"Hold it, Schultz. Don't move, you're under arrest."

Freeman didn't laugh as his new name was changed from Swartz to Schultz. From then on in the script, Swartz became Schultz.

By the time DeBrock did arrive, it was too late to start over again. Besides, I had used up all the snow. I now became the "introductory" star of *Protectors of the Outdoors.* The director and the photographer promised they'd someday show me the parts of the movie they cut out. Maybe there is an old reel on those DNR shelves we could all laugh at. To this day, I haven't seen the swan dives on film.

There is a final episode to this true but humiliating story about my movie career. The director, it turned out, lived in my wife's hometown.

One of my brothers-in-law attended a department movie at the church one night. It was put on by the DNR and shown by the director, who also belonged to the church (small world). As the director was setting up the projector and the screen, he couldn't resist telling the audience about the northern Wisconsin warden who had almost made the movie into a comedy. He told them how all the moviemakers laughed as this warden did tailspins into the snow and turned Swartz into Schultz with a flick of the tongue.

"I have a brother-in-law by the name of Dave Swendsen who's a warden in northern Wisconsin. Do you know him?" asked my brother-in-law.

"Do I *know* him, do I *know* him!"

PART II

SEVERAL YEARS
INTO THE FRAY

All kinds of people make a path

When does a person stop being a rookie in his or her profession? I will always feel like a rookie in some ways. There is so much to learn about the wilderness, about wildlife, and about the many kinds of human beings that use the outdoors. But I think there is a time of seasoning we all go through in our selected vocations. Once I had been through some of the tough days and nights, making mistakes and looking foolish, next time around I'd been there. I had experience that could never be gained or absorbed from books. I guess you step from the rookie stage when you stop making the same mistakes twice.

After two or three years in my northwoods station—wrestling with deer shiners, getting stuck ten miles from nowhere, losing many cases which I thought were open and shut, and working hours that only an obsessed gold miner would understand—I think I could consider myself no longer a rookie. Yes, still a long way to go toward veteran status, but my seasoning was coming the hard way. I guess I feel like Bill Waggoner did when he said, "Tough times, I wouldn't go through that again for love or money—yet I wouldn't want to have missed the experience."

Now that my rookie days were behind me, learning what makes people tick, in the outdoors, was my next stepping-stone toward being a professional wildlife officer. The next five or six years didn't give me all the answers, but they sure raised more questions.

Almost everyone uses the outdoors. I soon found that few know much about it. I also found that almost everyone will violate at least some fish, game, or outdoor regulations. Now don't be shocked. Most people will also violate traffic regulations under certain conditions and frames of mind.

I can tell you about some professional football players, honor students, old women, police officers, bankers, factory owners, detectives, and public officials who decided they would violate an outdoor regulation. Yes, lawyers, ministers, mayors, and priests—although not usually prone to do so—sometimes become involved in fish and game regulation improprieties. Campers, hikers, hunters, fishermen, and other wilderness users—regardless of age, race, educational background, or status in life—still appear to be only people, people pretty much like you and me. Under certain conditions these people will speed or try to beat a yellow light. But it is not every driver who will drink and drive.

On occasion, some hunters will shoot after hours or take an extra duck over the limit. Not every hunter would steal someone else's deer or shine or shoot a doe with fawns. In my early days as a warden, I found that people's past experience, their family background and training, and their mood of the day determine what they will do when the opportunity to violate a fish or game law comes along. Let me tell you a story about the labels *slobs* and *white knights*. Afterward, you decide what you think of such labels.

Late one September evening, two men drove to the edge of a fresh cut clover field in northern Wisconsin. A rifle barrel slid out the side window as one of the men trained a 30-30 on the large deer that was grazing quietly at the far end of the field. The big doe accompanied by her two fawns had been routinely feeding in this field since June, when the fawns were born. The men knew the deer would be there. They had plans for this deer.

Just across the road, a farmer's wife watched with anger rising within her. She stood at her kitchen window powerless to do anything about what was about to happen. Her husband had gone to town for cattle feed. They had been watching and enjoying the three deer for several months.

The woman heard a muffled shot and the big doe slumped to the ground. The two startled fawns raised their heads, waiting for their mother to lead them to safety. Just then the two men jumped from their running car and dashed toward the fallen doe. The two fawns, their tails flagging, scampered off into the temporary safety of the nearest pines.

The deer season was closed. A special permit is required to shoot does. It is also illegal to shoot from a vehicle. All three Wisconsin regulations were violated, with more to follow as the two men picked up the deer. Slob hunters?

Not far away on a clear, calm, pine-fringed lake, a man and a young boy fish. They cast their own hand-tied poppers carefully and precisely into the widening rings left by a big feeding smallmouth bass. The bass had just sucked up a floundering bug and was rolling back toward the cover of some nearby lily pads.

The boy let his popper hit the quiet water lightly and then twitched his rod tip just right. That action sent the frog-colored lure hopping lifelike toward the lily pads. The big bass couldn't resist. She swung around and charged this second course of the evening menu, and before the "frog" had gone two feet, she grabbed it and headed for the bottom. As soon as the big bass felt the hook, she went straight into the air, with water flying in all directions. By the time the twelve-year-old boy led the five-pound fighter carefully into the net held by his father, five exciting minutes had passed. Those five minutes were filled with joy and accomplishment and a special irreplaceable experience between a father and a son.

The young boy carefully removed the hook from the lip of the big-eyed female bass as it lay exhausted, safely inside the confines of the net webbing.

"It's Old Monster, Dad." The boy hesitated for a moment and then said softly, "I'm going to put her back. What would fishing be like in this part of the lake without Old Monster still around?" The father winked and rolled the net over as his son gently pushed the big fish back into the quiet depths.

Watching with my binoculars from a hundred yards away, I knew that their licenses, boat registration, bag limits, and life preservers would all be in order. Were these two sportsmen as pure as the driven snow? Were they white knights?

You would probably rate the first two outdoor abusers as slobs. The boy and his father would probably be rated by almost everyone as true sportsmen, capable of no wrong. But as a young wildlife officer, I wasn't too quick to judge those I approached and sometimes arrested in the outdoors.

Supervisor Waggoner had warned me not to put all fish and game and wilderness users in the same basket. I also had to learn not to put all violators in the same basket. My last several years of enforcing the wildlife laws had begun to teach me that there are violators who have made mistakes, some with and some without knowledge of what they are doing.

But there are also people who lie awake at night, figuring out a way to break the fish and game laws. These premeditative outlaws, in my short experience, appeared to be a small percentage of the outdoor-user population, just as those persons who never seemed to violate any wildlife laws looked to me like a very small segment.

I'd like to take you along with me on some of my contacts and confrontations. You'll see that some of these people—whether they were house painters, policemen, or pharmacists—could act crudely or small when arrested. Even during some very embarrassing times, others could stand tall and show what kind of stuff they were made of.

In our journeys, the labels *slobs* and *white knights* will appear and reappear. I hope, as you and I meet the many different kinds of people described in the chapters of this book, we will learn about and understand the danger of judging anyone too quickly.

Doctor, lawyer, Indian chief

Time to learn again: A person's profession doesn't necessarily govern his actions in the outdoors any more than one's conduct can be predicted by his weight or height. I now had several years of people experience under my warden belt. How would you have reacted to this encounter? July, 1958.

Doctor

No rookie, but still learning. I decided to check fishermen on a small Wisconsin lake. It was a lake I figured might never have had a warden on it. Sometimes those who fish such a lake become careless about purchasing a license.

Back in a little cove at the far end of the lake, I could see a man and a woman fishing. They were the only fishermen on the lake. After watching through my binoculars for a few minutes to be sure they were both fishing, I put in my boat and motored slowly toward them.

"Good morning, I'm a conservation warden. I'd like to see your fishing licenses."

The man told me he was a doctor from Minneapolis. He said he came to Wisconsin every year for a few weeks' vacation. He and his wife spent a lot of money while in the area, enjoying their time away from the big-city life.

"Must have left the licenses back at the cabin," the doctor said as he examined his billfold for the second time.

"Where are you staying, doctor? I'm about through here on the lake, maybe we can go take a look at the licenses back at your cabin."

We ended up motoring back to the boat landing, loading our boats, and driving about ten miles to another lake where the couple had rented a cabin. I waited at my car as the doctor and his wife went to the cabin to get their licenses. They were gone for some time.

The doctor finally came out again and apologized for the inconvenience. He said the licenses must be in his car. He then spent ten minutes searching diligently through the car. His wife came out with her purse, which she searched through carefully. Still no licenses. After a final pocket searching by both of them, they threw up their hands and looked at me. The license search would have put a Russian border guard to shame. Until now, there hadn't been any indication that there were no licenses.

I asked the doctor where he had purchased his non-resident licenses and how much he had paid for them. These were questions I would have asked much earlier, had they shown any indication that they might not have purchased them. The doctor became more nervous and a little belligerent when he saw I wasn't going to just go away like a bad cold. He suddenly looked a little sick.

"Tell him George. This has gone too far," said his wife. He shook his head sadly, as if he had just been caught robbing the bank.

"We don't have any licenses. I forgot to get them when we arrived last Sunday. My wife kept telling me to go to town and get the licenses. I was just telling her how I had been fishing this lake for years and had never seen a warden—just then you motored around the point and I knew you had to be a warden. Truthfully, I thought you'd give up and not pursue the matter so diligently."

I'm sure the doctor's penalty was much more painful at home than it was in court. I bet the doctor's wife is still reminding him of "the wardens who never check this lake for licenses."

Lawyer

Up until now, most of my cases had been handled easily in court. My defendants, except for Tom Balto the fur dealer, had posted a bond at the sheriff's office, pleaded guilty and paid a small fine, or had been found not guilty by the local municipal judge. But I was about to receive another kind of education. This next lesson, usually learned by north-woods wardens in the first few years of their existence, was called *defense lawyer*.

In our county, there were only about a half-dozen attorneys. Two of them were judges. One was the county prosecutor. The rest belonged to a three-man firm that defended all clients charged with game-law violations. The most frequent violators were usually prepared to pay an attorney rather than pay their fine.

Unfortunately, the only defense attorney firm in our county was made up of attorneys who usually won their cases. Their office sign was a painful truth: PAY YOUR FINE, OR PAY US TO PROVE YOU INNOCENT. Past history had proven their sign to be right; fish and game cases hardly ever got to a jury trial.

My supervisor was honest with me. He told me there hadn't been a successful fish or game jury trial in our county for years.

I had arrested two well-known violators who had, for years, lived off the land with little respect for others, little respect for wildlife, and no respect for game wardens. I watched Joe and Earl for over an hour. They used nine tipups as they caught three- and four-pound walleyed pike through the ice. (Wisconsin law allowed only two tipups apiece.)

I had parked my car far down the road and hiked quietly through the snow to my vantage point in a clump of shoreline birch, just sixty yards from the two lone fishermen on this secluded lake. I was there because other fishermen had complained to me that Joe and Earl fished every day, caught way over their five-fish-apiece limit, and always used more than two tipups.

It was late afternoon and a few flakes of snow began to drift down past the hazy sun when I decided I had seen enough to establish that Joe and Earl were fishing with too many lines. My notes indicated that I had seen Joe handle and land fish with four lines, and Earl had used five. I recorded how they were dressed and the exact time each man used a particular tipup. I had mapped and numbered them all in my notes.

By the time I left my vantage point, it was beginning to turn dark and the snow started to come down just a little more heavily. But as I confronted Joe and Earl, visibility was no problem. We picked up all the fishing gear and twelve large walleyes. I proceeded to take down all the information and write each a citation to appear in court.

"Other fishermen were here earlier in a four-wheel drive," said Joe, not knowing how long I had observed them. "They left the extra lines and drove off the lake an hour before you arrived."

It was each man's third offense; a conviction would possibly cost them their licenses. I knew they would fight the case in court. I was right.

Joe and Earl asked for a jury trial and hired Glen Reed as their attorney. Reed was the oldest, most experienced member of the local firm of Reed, Parker & Johnson. After almost three years as the local warden, I was ready to attend my first jury trial. I was concerned about all I had heard about fish and game jury trials, but I felt I had a good case.

Glen Reed whistled through his teeth when he addressed the court. But because of his bearing and courtroom experience, no one laughed. I didn't.

When Reed had me on the stand, he drilled me about the time and conditions of the day of the fishing. I described it as late afternoon, few flakes of snow—enough visibility to easily identify and even write up the defendants.

As Reed summed up his presentation to the jury, I watched my whole case go down the drain.

When Glen finished his summation, the jury must have wondered how I had been able to "identify" from "six hundred yards away" (Glen added a zero but no one corrected him) the two innocent farmers, "with the setting sun in my eyes," then "in the black of night" with "a raging snowstorm blotting out my vision and judgment."

The jury found Joe and Earl not guilty. Glen Reed went on whistling through his teeth and winning. I had to give back the illegally taken walleyes—then I went back to the drawing board. I had learned another hard lesson. To quote an old-time warden from Minnesota: "There ain't no such thing as an open and shut case, regardless of the evidence."

Indian chief

In only a few short years as a wildlife officer, I had to apprehend or arrest farmers, some high school athletes, my neighbor's brother, a little old grandmother, and a city clerk. But then came the Indian chief. Let me tell you about him; you'll like him.

I received an emergency call on my two-way radio late one afternoon during the nine-day deer season. Two of my forest ranger deputies were calling for help. The radio call, relayed through the ranger station, was a message that the rangers had run into thirty Indians making a deer drive down the middle of a state wildlife refuge.

I arrived at the scene only a few minutes later. As I approached the rangers' truck, I saw thirty armed, irate men swarming around the

two rangers. Some of these men had bottles and appeared to be intoxicated. I could see a scalping was about to take place.

Spreading a cloud of dust over the scene, I skidded my car to a
stop in the middle of the uprising, my red light flashing. I bounded out
of my car and stepped between the rangers and the angry Indians.

"Who's the chief here?" I asked, not knowing what else to say.

Everyone became quiet. The Indians looked around at each other
in an openmouthed manner.

"Joe—Joe Bearclaw there," said one of the hunters, pointing to
a surprised little old man at the edge of the war party. "He's the chief."

"Yeh," several others joined in, "Joe—he's the chief."

With little Ed's words still ringing in my ears—"always attack,
never retreat"—I said, "Chief Bearclaw, tell your men to take their
guns and go over and sit down along the fence. You, please, come over
and sit in my car with me and we'll discuss this hunting misunder-
standing between your men and the rangers."

All of a sudden, Chief Bearclaw, who I am sure had never been
called chief before, stepped forward and said loudly, "All right, men,
go over and sit down. I'll talk this over with the warden."

"Tell your men they had better carefully unload their weapons
and lay them down in front of them so that no one gets hurt," I said
quickly. "And tell them to get out their hunting licenses so the rangers
can look at them while you and I are settling this matter."

Chief Bearclaw gave the order and to my surprise and the rangers'
relief, every man, one by one, began to unload his rifle. The chief and
I got into my car. I watched as the rangers started writing down names
and addresses as the licenses started to come out.

The chief told his men he had convinced me that if I allowed them
to go home now, he would see that all would appear in court the next
day regarding the "mix-up" of hunting in a state wildlife refuge. He
also told his men to allow the rangers to pick up all the guns, which
would be returned to them the next day by the judge.

Once we had all the guns in the rangers' truck, and all the names
of the hunters, I shook hands with Chief Bearclaw and told him he
could send his men home.

"All right men, you can go home now," said the chief, relishing
his new importance, as any of us might. They went, still looking a little
baffled at their new chief's leadership abilities.

Thirty sober Indians pleaded guilty the next day to hunting deer
in a state wildlife refuge. They each agreed to pay a small fine and
received a warning from the astonished judge about hunting in refuges
and drinking while carrying guns. The guns were returned as promised.

The judge was truly surprised when the thirty Indians nodded their approval as one man spoke for all of them. The spokesman? Who else, but a little old man named Chief Joe Bearclaw.

A man of character

Arresting your neighbor is not a pleasant task. Just how difficult it may be depends a lot on the neighbor. I'd like to tell you about a neighbor of mine. When the chips were down, I found out not just how someone reacts when he is tempted in the outdoors, but I also found out how a man can be a man when it gets down to him and me and the badge.

Wildlife officers check millions of fishermen each year. These fishermen are people like you and your neighbor, and my neighbor too. People of all descriptions and backgrounds go fishing. A majority of the fishermen who are checked by wildlife officers have violated no regulations.

As might be expected, most people don't go out fishing with the intention to violate the fishing laws and regulations. Most are pretty darn careful. But when the conditions are tempting, a large proportion of those who do fish will bend or break certain fishing regulations.

"I only get out on opening day. So I guess I feel I am entitled to take two days' limit of fish at one time." That's an excuse I have heard many times. A nice guy and his two friends took double their limit of big walleyed pike one opening day in Wisconsin. The nice guy was my neighbor.

The undersheriff called me at about 11 P.M. on the opening day of the fishing season. He had information that one of our neighbors and his two fishermen friends had "showed off" thirty big walleyes (fifteen over their limit) that evening. The undersheriff, Dale Morey, now a warden in charge of boat safety in Wisconsin, said that another citizen had seen the fish. We agreed it would be hard to find the fishermen or the fish at such a late hour. I decided to wait until morning.

The undersheriff, our overbag fisherman neighbor, and I all lived on a dead-end road on the same beautiful lake. There was also a small airport and a nice tavern-restaurant on this road between our houses and the main part of town. I knew several things the undersheriff didn't know that made me decide to wait to visit my overbag neighbor, Jim, until morning.

I knew Jim was a pilot who lived most of the year in Illinois. He had his summer home on the lake, which he and his friends flew to for the opening of the fishing season. I also knew there was a fly-in breakfast planned at the tavern-restaurant the next morning. I knew Jim and his friends would be eating pancakes there bright and early before they loaded up their fish and flew home to Illinois.

I also knew Jim was a pretty nice guy. He was a trout fisherman who had come to my house one day and asked me, "Can you tell me where I can go catch a trout?" Jim and I then sat at my picnic table, took out a green-line map, and I showed him how to get to streams where I had planted trout.

After talking to Jim for about an hour, I could tell he was my kind of trout fisherman. He would get that little twinkle in his eye when he talked about how to outwit the big browns. He wasn't just after a full bag. The next time I talked to Jim about trout fishing, I told him how to get to some of my favorite secluded streams, ones I didn't plant. They had native fish. He came back later to tell me about some of the good fish he caught or lost in those special pools.

Now Jim was in trouble with me. At about 7 A.M., I parked my patrol car along the road between Jim's cabin and the tavern-restaurant. It was easy for Jim and his two fishing companions to saunter up to breakfast at 6 A.M. and walk back to Jim's cabin by 7 A.M. or so. In a short time, they could be back at their cabin, ready for their return home. They could then carry their gear and fish across the road to the airport and fly back to Illinois by late afternoon.

I watched until I saw Jim and his two companions, full of pancakes and coffee, coming down the road. They passed right by my car. (I was in uniform.)

"Hi, Jim. Could I see you for a moment?"

Jim came over to the window. I asked him if he would climb in for a minute. He motioned his friends along and told them he would meet them back at the cabin. Jim looked embarrassed as he slid into the seat beside me.

"I'm going to get straight to the point, Jim, and I feel you'll be honest with me as you and I have been honest with each other in the past." I looked him straight in the eye. "I understand you and your two friends got carried away with the excellent fishing success yesterday and came away with twice as many walleyes as the law allows? I know this is the second day and you could tell me that you went out at midnight and caught the second limit, but I don't think you'll lie to me. What happened, Jim?"

"You heard right," Jim said without hesitating. "We got carried away pulling in big walleyes, biggest I've caught on the lake. We knew we were going home today and wouldn't be able to fish today. So I guess I decided that somehow we were entitled to the second limit. We were wrong. Dave, what do we do now?''

"Well, Jim, I guess the best and quickest way to clear this up would be to make a trip to the sheriff's office. You and your friends can post a bond for a plea of nolo.'' (*Nolo contendere* means not contesting the charges held against a person.)

"Let's go do it, Dave.''

"We'll need the fish.''

"OK, I'll get them for you.''

Jim and I walked to the lakeside door of his cabin. His two friends looked astonished as Jim led me into the front room, where they sat waiting to return to Illinois with their wonderful catch of big walleyes. Jim led me past his bug-eyed companions to the refrigerator and proceeded to pull out walleye fillets plus fifteen in-the-round fish, some as large as seven pounds. While his two companions watched in disbelieving silence, Jim loaded the thirty fish into a large cardboard box and told his friends to carry the fish out to my car.

In twenty minutes we were all at the sheriff's office, and Jim and his two friends posted bond for $50 apiece. Jim's friends asked me what was going to happen to the fish. I told them they would be sold by the state or given to a hospital or old folk's home. They wondered if they could buy some of the fish. I told them I would check with the judge. The judge agreed on the phone that I could sell, under state red tag, one limit of fish per defendant. I sold them the fish in-the-round, for the going rate of $1.25 per pound.

As Jim was leaving the sheriff's office, he stopped and shook my hand.

"Well, Dave, I'm sorry this happened. I don't suppose you'll ever trust me again.''

"Jim, the way you handled this situation and your friends has convinced me I can *always* trust you. Come see me when you get up this summer and we'll go find a trout hole together. Now you go explain to your friends why you did what you did today. I'll bet they're dying to hear your story.''

Years later, Jim and I did fish trout together. Jim was a man of character.

My faith in juveniles

It was very dark. There were three of them. By now they must have speared ten or twelve big walleyes from out of the culvert that ran under the road. I was too far away to see every move, but I knew from what I had seen and from the noises of the spear banging on the side of the culvert that their car would be moving in my direction soon.

I could now see them starting to move. I heard a car door slam, then a second and a third. Soon the car was rolling toward me. Since I was alone, I decided to let it pass, drop in behind, and stop it with the red light and siren.

I jumped into my hidden car just as the outlaw car rolled by me and threw on its lights. I dropped in behind, my lights out, watching for a good stopping spot. After about a mile I was surprised to see the car slow down and wheel off into a little dead-end road. I thought, good, it will make a stop easier for me. But as I followed the car down the narrow drive, I remembered there was another small stream that usually ran walleyes on this road too. Sure enough, they were going to stop at the stream just ahead. I decided I would make my move before they got out and started into the stream.

Just as their car hit its brake lights and became dark, I threw on the siren and red light and bounded out of the car. When I approached the driver's side with my big flashlight, my piercing light exposed three somewhat startled teenagers, unable to move from their seats. I took the keys from the driver and said, "Get out of the car and stand alongside. You are under arrest." I found a bag of nice fat spawning walleyes in the trunk, and a spearhead on the floor of the front seat. It was wet and bloody.

The young men were quite cooperative. I soon had two in the car with me and the driver following me back to their hometown at the far end of the eighteen-mile-long lake we were paralleling.

While we drove along, I talked to the boys about their thrills of the night. They told my they had to spear walleyes off the Slim Creek culvert if they wanted to belong, to be accepted in their junior class at high school. "Everyone did it at least once; it was traditional."

I asked the two boys if they had ever been in jail before. They replied, "No sir." I said quietly, "You know, boys, it's traditional that wardens put fish spearers in jail when they're caught with spawning walleyes." I went on to explain to them about how long it takes to grow a seven-pound walleye, and how much these fish mean to the economy of the people in their town, a resort area.

I drove straight to the judge's house. I got him out of bed. I brought the three boys in and sat them down at the judge's kitchen table. I told the judge about the junior class tradition these boys were participating in. He was very understanding. He proceeded to give the young men, whom he knew, a lecture.

When the judge finished, I asked him if I could make a suggestion. I asked him if I could be assigned these young men for the rest of the spearing season, to help me patrol the streams. He looked at me in surprise, but gave his permission, instead of binding them over to county court.

I told the boys I expected them at the sheriff's office the next day bright and early. Then we called their parents and had them come and pick the boys up.

"If your sons don't cooperate with the warden, I will have them back before me within the week," the judge told them.

The three boys—Tim, Gary, and Fred— met me at the sheriff's office on time the next morning. I took them to several streams where we met the fish truck and planted trout. I then took them to the fish hatchery where spawning walleyes had been brought in to strip eggs so that fry could be raised for planting in lakes where reproduction was off. We also visited the conservation commissioner who lived in the county seat; he told the boys how important these fish were to the state and their town.

For more than a dozen nights the three boys rode with me as I checked streams, checked people, and apprehended spearers. Soon they found themselves thinking from the other side of the fence. When I took them back to see the judge several weeks later, it appeared our experiment had worked. The boys told the judge they never realized the importance and wonder of these spawning fish—and the long hard hours that wardens worked to protect the fish for the public.

One year later I was in the boys' town, at the high school. I had just given a gun safety demonstration to the senior class and felt it had been well-received. As always, a group of students gathered around me as I put away my equipment.

Three seniors came through to the front. They had something to tell me. It was Tim, Gary, and Fred. They were wearing jackets with an emblem. The emblem read Conservation Club.

They told me how they had started the club after their experience with me and how they recruited other students to stand guard at some of the local spearing spots when the walleyes were running. They had become very concerned about the wildlife. They also said they had helped to change the old tradition at their school. No longer was it so neat and smart to spear fish at the Slim Creek culvert. Fred told me

During his service in Wisconsin, Swendsen for three years was in charge of a program called Conservation Day. Here, as part of that program, he demonstrates gun safety to high-school students in Drummond. Schedule called for visiting each high school in 12-county area at least once every four years, talking to juniors or seniors.

that students who still speared fish weren't popular; they were reported to the local sheriff's deputy by club members.

"I'll never forget the two weeks we spent with you," Tim said. "It changed my whole outlook on wildlife and wild things."

Gary, the club president, asked, "Would you attend our next meeting and give a little talk to our thirty-five members on how people must help to protect the wildlife they care about?"

How could I refuse?

"*My God, Harvey, you shot the SOB!*"

My assistant supervisor and our warden pilot had hidden themselves on a small knoll in the woods. They were looking down directly onto a big bend in the rushing stream. The waters twisted and cut their way through the heavy Wisconsin timber. In those waters were thousands of fat spawning walleyes.

I waited in my patrol car, keeping in contact with Harvey and Earle through their portable radio. Our plan was for me to be able to report road traffic and stop escaping cars that might be loaded with walleyed pike. My car was pulled up off the main road on an old logging trail. I had covered the car with my old dyed parachute, so it wouldn't be spotted from the bridge.

Harvey and Earle reported lots of fish churning their way up the stream to spawn. Seven- to thirteen-pound females and thinner, but more numerous males, pushed their way upstream through the riffles to produce fry for next year's fishing, or maybe the year after. We were there to see that some of the fish made it up and back.

Our information made sense. A resort owner, whose livelihood depended indirectly on these fish (providing fishing for his guests who bought bait, rented boats, and equipment), told us that some of the local boys had been bragging about the big pike they were netting out of Phantom Creek, just down from the old Wilson bridge.

"There are two guys in the stream just below us," Harvey called on the radio. "They have a big landing net. Looks like they came upstream from the old cemetery road. They probably have a car parked there now."

I told him I would check it out. We would stay in radio contact. I found a car parked on the cemetery road. There was someone in the car smoking a cigarette. I got close enough on foot to get the license number from the car and then hurried back to my radio.

I got back just in time to hear Harvey say, "We're moving in on the netters." I said I would keep track of the car and the driver. Then there was radio silence.

Harvey related the story to me later that night, and again before the county judge in trial two weeks later.

"Just as Earle and I started down the bank toward the netters, the handle on their net must have broken. They probably tried to get more fish in the net than it could handle in the fast water. Wet and swearing, the two men came out of the stream carrying their broken net and their gunnysack almost full of fish. They came out before we were in a position to grab them.''

I'll relate the rest of Harvey's story, which went something like this: When the spearers saw the wardens, they dropped everything and ran. The younger man ran down the stream toward the cemetery.

"You're under arrest," Earle shouted, and gave chase. Harvey's man turned back toward the stream, hesitated for a split second, and then plunged feet first into the three- to four-foot-deep water of the pool, just above where the two men had been taking fish. In only a few seconds the heavy-set man, dressed in a red and black plaid shirt, waded quickly across the pool and started to scurry up the steep bank on the other side of the stream.

Earle's man had given him the slip, at least for now. Earle came back hoping to catch the second netter. Earle described what he saw when he got back to the pool:

"As I had just about reached the pool, I heard Harvey shout, 'Stop, or I'll shoot!' Then I heard two quick explosions, *Ka boom, Ka boom!* I hurried even faster to the pool's edge. I saw Harvey standing at the edge of the water, his drawn, smoking revolver in the air. I looked quickly across the pool as I heard a cry and the plaid-shirted netter was tumbling backwards, ending up splashing into the cold water. I called out, 'My God, Harvey, you shot the SOB!' ''

But when old Plaid Shirt hit the forty-five-degree water, he came alive. He hadn't been shot. No bullet had come anywhere near him. Harvey had shot into the air, but at that exact time, Plaid Shirt caught his foot on a tree root in the bank and fell backwards.

Earle and Harvey quickly placed Plaid Shirt under arrest. I latched onto the other netter and the car lookout just as the second netter came back and jumped into the waiting car.

Backwoods justice isn't always what we think it ought to be. The county judge found the netters not guilty of taking walleyes during the closed season. He was not happy with Earle's excited cry out on the spawning stream, "My God, Harvey, you shot the SOB!" These are words Earle will never forget. And whether the netters had actually been netting fish out of Phantom Creek didn't seem to matter to the judge. He turned them loose.

"My dad always has a license."

Many people abuse the wilderness. Their inconsiderate acts are often due to apathy or an upbringing which was void of outdoor tutelage or discipline. But, like father, like son can work both ways. A person's respect for wild things and places can be passed on to one's children, just as a lack of respect is sometimes passed on. Read on and you will meet a man who wanted his children to love the wilderness as he did.

One day I happened to check a man and two boys as they fished a secluded Wisconsin lake where wardens seldom roamed. I had, as usual, watched for awhile with my binoculars to be sure that the man was actually fishing. I had decided to go to this lake because it was a super bass lake and the bass season was not yet open. These three fishermen did not really look like the culprits I thought I might find under such circumstances, but legal fishermen deserve to be checked out too. I have checked old men who say, "I've been fishing for fifty years and you are the first warden to look at my license."

I motored up quietly to the three fishermen, shut off my motor, and said, "Good morning, I'm a conservation warden. How's your luck? Could I please see your fishing license?" (The boys were too young to need one.)

I could see a stringer of bluegills hanging from the side of their boat. I will have to admit I really expected these fishermen to have a few bass. It was right in the height of the spawning season and I had seen bass spawning nests (small round depressions hollowed out by the big fish) all along the shoreline. It was an awful temptation.

"Look at our fish," volunteered the younger boy, as he held up the stringer of flopping bluegills. The man had set down his pole and was digging through his billfold for his license. My eyes were carefully scanning the boat for other fish or other stringers or lines on which an out-of-season bass might be tied. Sometimes an illegal fish might be placed on a handy line that could be cut quickly as a warden approached. The father was still looking for his license.

Now the older boy, only about nine or ten years old, looked at my badge and the fish and said proudly, "My dad always has a license. He teaches us always to obey the law."

The other boy quickly added, "Dad made me put back the biggest bass I ever saw." He held his hands about twenty inches apart and went on with his story. "Dad showed us that the big fish was a mother and was full of eggs. So we put her back so she could have babies. Dad said we could come back and try to catch her again next month when the bass season opens. Boy, did she ever put up a fight."

I could see the boys' father had finally found his fishing license in his billfold and was waiting to hand it to me.

"From what your sons have been telling me, sir, I know your license is in order. You can put it away. I'm glad to see that you're teaching your boys that there is more to fishing than catching fish."

The man smiled and winked. I'm sure he was pleased to see his sons' reaction to meeting a warden on the lake.

I spent the next hour showing the boys how they could see the big bass guarding their nests. We rowed carefully along the shore and looked down through my Polaroid sunglasses. Their excitement made the day for their father and for me.

I knew when I left this man and his two sons that none of us had wasted our time that morning. I was sure that the boys' respect for their father and his fisherman honesty had been proved as the right way to go. It was something worthy of passing on from father to son. The big spawning bass had a chance with fishermen like these. I believe that with more fathers and sons like these, not only the fish and the wilderness, but the world will stand a better chance of survival.

In his book, *Conservation Saga,* Ernie Swift talked about the young and the outdoors. He wrote,

When and where does conservation education begin? Where SHOULD it begin? Does it start with emotions that swell the childish breast at the first conscious sight of a butterfly, a robin, a dandelion, a field of daisies, a lonely pasqueflower, or mud oozing up between bare toes? Is it awakened when a father takes his son hunting or fishing? Does it begin with cows being driven to pasture, or with day-dreaming along the banks of a small water course? Does it begin in the school room, or the more matter-of-fact problem of finding a job? . . . the conservation conscience must begin with the young, and there should be opportunity for the blooming. In the end it will keep the *old* young at heart. It should start in adolescence with emotions and avid curiosity and should progress with study, research and contemplation. But emotions should never be discarded. An open mind with an insatiable curiosity are the two main avenues to conservation education, because in the last analysis conservation education must have balance and produce an understanding between man and the land. As Aldo Leopold has so well stated, "Genuine curiosity can only be satisfied by working directly with the land, water, and the products of both. There is no substitute. These are the elements which make up the whole of conservation."

I suspect if we wait too long to teach our eager, caring, curious children, they will become apathetic, uncaring, and unknowing adults— adults with the future of the world in their hands.

Honker Davis

Arresting a friend's minister wasn't an enjoyable task. The minister really was a nice guy, but like most of us, not infallible. But let me start at the beginning.

I received a phone call one evening from a very reliable citizen. He said he had some information for me that he overheard while picking up a case of beer at a local pub. I drove over to the informant's house a few minutes later. When I arrived he gave me this information:

One of the men at the bar was a farmer who lived just a few miles south of town. The farmer couldn't help but tell this exciting story of how the migrating geese landed in his pond. The big birds, which usually flew over very high and seldom landed, "came down plum in the middle of my tame goose pond. About a hundred of them came a-honking and a-splashing into the pond right near our house." Others at the bar wanted to know, were they still there?

"Oh no," said the farmer, "no sooner did the geese drop down into the pond and over the hill came two guys creeping on them with their shotguns."

Everyone, including my friend, wanted to know if they got any.

"Boy, did they get into them," exclaimed the farmer. "They crept up closer and closer until the two men lay almost at the water's edge. I was watching them from the barn. Then they jumped up and emptied their shotguns point blank into the flock of tired geese, before the big birds could lift their bodies back up into the air.

"Man alive," the farmer cried, "there were feathers and crippled geese flopping and cackling and going in all directions."

"How many did they get, George?" Everyone wanted to know.

"I'm not sure," replied the farmer, "but the two hunters brought four big honkers up to the house and gave them to my wife. Looks like goose for dinner next Sunday at our place."

As my friend was leaving the pub, he heard the farmer mention the name of one of the goose hunters. Then he went home and called me.

I arrived at the home of the hunter about twenty minutes later. I was just in time to meet him coming out of his garage with a big bag of goose feathers, his hands bloody, and his expression one of surprise. I asked Harry to get me the geese. Dejectedly he came out with four freshly picked and cleaned Canada geese. The limit was two.

"Harry, let's you and I take a ride, first out to the farm. Then to see your hunting companion."

The farmer's wife was also surprised when Harry and I knocked on the door. Her hands were bloody and goose feathers were all over her apron. In a short time, she and her husband loaded their four geese in a box and handed it to me. I told them I would not press charges, but would be back to talk to them later.

Our next stop was back in town. I asked Harry to tell me where to find his hunting companion. He didn't want to tell me.

"Harry, I'm going to find out anyway. It would be better for all of you if you would just take me to his house."

Harry shook his head sadly, and then told me to drive to the top of the hill. I followed his directions until I found myself parked in front of the church.

"Come on now, Harry. It's not Sunday. Where from here?" He pointed to the parsonage next door and again shook his head.

"Harry, you mean your partner was Reverend Davis?"

Just then I saw Reverend Davis come out of his house and walk toward his garage and garbage can. Guess what he was carrying!

Early the next morning I received a call. I recognized the voice right away.

"Dave, I understand you arrested my wife's minister last night."

"Yes, John, I did. He just happened to go goose hunting for the first time in his life and the hunting was too good. You know, the temptation was too much. He really is a pretty nice guy. He and Harry have already posted bond at the sheriff's office. I've turned the geese over to the hospital for a Sunday meal for the patients. I thought Reverend Davis would approve of that."

"Yes, I know," John said with a wee bit of a chuckle. "Do you know what they're calling the Reverend?"

"No, I haven't heard anything about that."

Again I thought I could hear a wee bit of a chuckle from his end of the phone.

"They're calling him Honker Davis."

Seeing is believing

Wildlife officers oftentimes hear some "wild people tales" that sound just too wild to be true. When such a tale involves them, they begin to learn that the more ridiculous the story, the more improbable it is that someone made it up.

For instance, another warden once told me about a man trolling with his fishing rod from the back of a horse. It couldn't be true, but I found out it was. And there's the story about a fisherman who lost his rod and reel over the side one year. While fishing a year later, his brother hooked onto the rod and retrieved the reel, only then to find it belonged to his brother.

And then my friend Tony, a trout fisherman, lost a huge steelhead trout when the fish broke his line after the line got tangled up with his dog. Somewhat perturbed with the dog, Tony later noticed a piece of fishing line lying across the large rock he was sitting on. It looked like his line. He tied the line onto his line from his reel and—yes, he landed the eight-pound trout. It had his spinner still in its mouth.

The story I am about to relate is just as crazy. It also is too unbelievable to be made up. In this case, fishermen prove they too are just people.

Wisconsin warden Glenn Chaffee and I were checking fishermen on Chetec Lake one Sunday afternoon when we noticed a pontoon boat with four people fishing on it. That particular boat first caught our attention because the four people—two men and two women—were running around, apparently fishing with a real frenzy. (We couldn't help but notice the two shapely young ladies. It was of course a warden's responsibility to observe all parties with our binoculars to determine exactly who was and who was not fishing.) The two attractive females and their two companions hardly looked up as Glenn and I motored up alongside their boat to check their fishing licenses.

Glenn and I noticed that the two young ladies seemed pretty inexperienced in their fishing efforts. They were trying to snag fish, but were dropping their obviously well-weighted lines over the side and then reefing their baits along the bottom. There were no fish to be snagged in this lake and certainly not at this time of year.

As we motored up to the boat, the two men set down their poles. All four of the fishermen were giggling. Glenn and I introduced ourselves and asked if the two couples would get out their fishing licenses.

"I don't think we need fishing licenses," said the blond woman, who was busy jerking her fishing pole up and down vigorously in the water.

I started to explain that all those who were sixteen years old and older, and those under seventy, needed a fishing license to fish in Wisconsin waters. The woman was obviously older than sixteen; and if she was seventy I would jump overboard.

"Do we need fishing licenses to fish for chickens?" asked the pretty brunette who dropped her line down again and gave it another hard tug. Then all four broke out laughing. One of the young men almost rolled on the floor of the boat. The other reached out and pulled our boat over. He thought it was time for him to explain the joke.

Just then, the blond said, "I've got one." Up came a soggy something from the bottom, wrapped in tinfoil. It was shaped like a chicken leg. One of the men began to explain.

"We came out today to play some bridge, have a few drinks, and cook our supper over the charcoal. We thought we would toss in our fishing lines just to add to the excitement. Everything was going fine. George had just bid six clubs, the lines were in the water, and I had just poured our second drink. Our charcoal cooker was all set up and the chickens, wrapped in tinfoil, were cooking away.

"Just then some boat jockey roared around the point with his big outboard going wide open. He was probably trying to impress the girls and get a better look. The boat roared away. The wake began to rock the pontoon boat. We didn't think anything of it. It had happened before.

"All of a sudden our charcoal burner on wheels started to roll to the other end of our boat. When it hit the railing on the other side, the chickens wrapped in tinfoil slid off the coals."

"Plunk, plunk," said the brunette. "Right into the water. Oh!" she screamed, "I've got one too."

She proceeded to pull a second chicken piece from the water with her big treble hooks attached to her line. By this time everyone was laughing, including two conservation wardens.

The men quickly put the chickens back on the fire and started to pour another drink to replace the ones spilled during the chicken dunk. The women now went to their purses and insisted on showing that they really had licenses. Their boyfriends had theirs too.

"Won't you have a drink with us?" one of the men asked.

"No thanks, some other time."

We started our motor and backed off slowly, so as not to rock their boat. The two couples waved as we headed for more fishermen. I could hear one of the girls say, "I'll bid six hearts, George." I heard George say, "I'll raise you two chickens."

More laughter carried across the water. I thought to myself, who's going to believe this story?

Neighbors have brothers

I have found that anyone can be a good neighbor when controversy or stress doesn't enter into the relationship. It is when problems and pressures arise between neighbors that their relationships are suddenly on the line. And when the pressure is on, our true character shows through.

Living near a wildlife officer can put certain pressures on people. Based on my many experiences with neighbors, I have decided that I have utmost faith that people will eventually do the right things toward their needed wilderness and its wildlife. My wife and I have lived in many places. I look back now and find that, without exception, our neighbors became our best friends.

All my neighbors and friends knew what my profession was, and none of them ever strained our friendship by expecting me to treat them differently than anyone else when wildlife law enforcement was involved. My neighbors always knew my standards about wildlife law enforcement. They knew the standards didn't change because of a person's status or our relationship.

Then there was Jim. I was checking duck hunters late one afternoon; in fact, it was just after the legal shooting hours. I heard shooting and made my way to the river bank where I thought I might get close enough to observe those doing the shooting. I was too late; the shooting stopped.

I was about to leave when I heard a canoe coming down the river. I saw two young men in the canoe. They were headed right for me. Their car was parked near mine, but they couldn't see me or the cars until they landed their canoe. I didn't think these two young men were the late shooters, as they had already put away their guns and had probably quit hunting on time. I thought it worth my efforts to wait and at least check out their licenses and bag limit.

I walked back up to my car to put away the old single-barrel shotgun I carried as a prop to look like a hunter. The two young men saw me and the cars about the time they landed. Soon they were dragging their boat up the path toward their car. They had left everything in their boat, but had left a wooden box behind a bush at the river's edge. I couldn't figure any good reason for them to leave the box down there unless there was something in it they didn't want someone to see. (Wardens can't help being suspicious.)

I walked down to meet the two young men and help them drag their loaded canoe to their car. I asked them how they did with their hunt. They said they had bagged their limit of mallards, two apiece.

They pulled out four nice mallards and showed me. I helped them load their gear and boat. I then checked their licenses.

One of the young men happened to be my neighbor's younger brother, Jim. He was only seventeen and a senior in high school. When Jim and his friend started to get into their car to leave, I got to the point.

"Jim, don't you want to walk back down and bring up the wooden box you left at the water's edge?"

"I hoped you wouldn't notice the box. Come on, I'll show it to you." Jim and I walked down to the river; his friend stayed back at the car.

"There's another mallard in the box. I'm sure you hear this a thousand times, but on my last shot, I hit two mallards. We already had three. So that put us over the limit. I didn't feel right leaving it there. When I saw your car, I just hoped you weren't a warden, but thought I would leave the extra bird in the box just in case." Jim turned over the box and out fell a mallard.

"Why don't you pick up your box and carry the mallard back to the cars, Jim."

He did, and as we walked back toward the parked cars, Jim said, "What makes me feel so bad is that my sister always told me what a nice guy you were and how I should meet you and talk about getting into conservation work, which I have always talked about doing. Now I have met you, and what a way to meet. I want you to know the extra mallard is mine, and my friend had nothing to do with taking it or hiding it."

"Jim, you didn't rob the First National Bank; you made a mistake. Might have been a little better if you hadn't hidden the bird, but I won't give you a lecture. As you know, I think a lot of your sister and her family, and we have talked about you and your education. Let's go from there. But first you'll have to straighten out your mistake about the extra mallard. We happen to be standing, not in my county, but in Burnette County. That means you have to go to Grantsburg to see the judge. Then we'll talk about your future in conservation work."

"Yes, sir, I'm prepared to take the consequences for the extra duck."

That night when I returned home, I walked over to see Jim's sister. She wasn't surprised to see me; Jackie and I were always popping in on her and her husband. I didn't know exactly how she would react to, "Hey, neighbor, I had to arrest your brother this afternoon."

I remembered my supervisor's famous words, "Blood is thicker than water." Bill had warned me many times that when you are dealing with someone's kinfolk, they just don't act the same as when it's not family. But I can remember Karen's words that night as if it were yesterday.

"So you had to arrest Jim. Good for you. He's been hanging around with some kids that he shouldn't hang around with. Maybe this will straighten that out. I hope he was a gentleman."

I assured her that he was. I told her I was going to drive him to Grantsburg for court. He would have to be excused from school that day. There was not a hint of sarcasm or anger then or ever in her attitude. Her husband's attitude and that of her whole family was top shelf about Jim's arrest.

I took Jim to court on Monday. He stood up before the judge like a man, with all the weekend drunks, car thieves, and traffic violators. He was fined $25.

I helped Jim get a temporary job with the conservation department working on forest fires. I gave him some guidance about schooling. He did go off to school to train for permanent work with the department. The episode showed Jim to be a man. It showed that my neighbors were made of the finer stuff. After graduating from college and going to work in the conservation field, Jim died tragically in an automobile accident. Jim was a man when he was still a boy; I will remember him that way.

Judges are people too

Remember the deer-shining, bed-stealing characters of the earlier chapter, "I put a gun in his ear"? Harold Kringle and Alden Monroe made their court appearances. As I related earlier, Alden pleaded guilty to stealing a bed and received one year's active probation. Harold pleaded guilty to hunting deer with an artificial light. He received a $100 fine, lost his hunting equipment, and was sentenced to 10 days in the county jail. Let me tell you what really happened.

The probation officer called me one day and asked whether I would accompany him to Alden's home. The judge had ordered that all of Alden's firearms be taken away during his probation and returned to him if Alden stayed out of trouble for a year. I said I would go.

We arrived at the Monroe home at about 3 P.M. It was a two-room house in which Alden and his wife lived with their nine children. Alden was cordial as he ushered us into the main room of the house with all of his family present. One wall was covered with firearms: shotguns, rifles, and even a revolver. After explaining to Alden what the judge had ordered and showing him the document, we started to take down the guns.

"Better be careful when you take down the guns," said Alden. "They're all loaded!"

"All loaded, with all these kids around?"

"Well, we all know it's the empty gun that kills people," he replied in all seriousness, "so I keep them all loaded."

Harold was offered a chance to serve his ten-day jail sentence under the Huber Law. The Huber Law allowed the sentenced party to get out of jail each day to work, but he had to be back in jail each night.

Allowing Harold to go to work in the daytime seemed a little unusual to me. Harold was a non-resident from Minnesota, and his job was across the state line seventy miles away. If Harold decided not to come back for the night, there wasn't much the state of Wisconsin could do. They seldom extradited people for misdemeanors.

After Harold's first night in jail, his construction boss arrived the next morning right on schedule to check him out for a Minnesota construction job. As the sheriff, the sheriff's wife, the deputy sheriff, and I all had expected, Harold didn't come back when the sun went down. He didn't come back after the second sun went down or the third either.

But after about six months, a strange thing happened. The sheriff's wife was sitting in the window of their office typing some case reports for her husband when she saw a sight she could hardly believe.

Two men were hobbling crazily up the street toward the city hall next door. The short man on the right was limping severely on his right leg. The tall, lean man on the left was limping and hobbling along on his left leg. It was a sight rarely seen on this earth.

These two men bobbing toward the city hall could be none other than Harold Kringle and Alden Monroe. (The sheriff's wife had seen both men before.) Alden Monroe had a gimpy right leg. He claimed he fell off a CCC truck back in the old days while fighting a big Wisconsin fire. Harold Kringle had a gimpy left leg, which I think he told me he hurt punching cows.

When Harold and Alden left the city hall a few minutes later, the sheriff was waiting for them at the door. Harold was invited to return to the jail to continue his visit of several months before. Harold and Alden were at the city hall to pick up some hunting licenses, which they could not legally buy, so I again became involved.

Even though Harold had in actuality escaped from jail when he didn't return from his job, the judge decided that he would only be required to serve his original ten days, but this time not under the Huber Law.

The sheriff's wife said she would never forget the sight of Alden and Harold coming toward her. When asked why Harold would take a chance of walking right up to the sheriff's office to get the fraudulent licenses, the two men said, "We didn't think anyone would notice us."

Maybe a change coming on

I had now been a Wisconsin conservation warden for about eight years. I loved my work. My wife and I had recently built a new home on the shores of beautiful Shell Lake. After years of waiting, we had within the last few years been blessed with an adopted son, and a daughter. I respected and liked my co-workers and my bosses. But now that I was thirty-three, I guess we decided some of the opportunities that seemed to be presenting themselves should be at least looked into.

Several of the U.S. Fish and Wildlife Service agents I frequently worked with suggested I take the federal exam. Ernie Swift, former Wisconsin warden, Wisconsin Conservation Department director, U.S. Fish and Wildlife Service Assistant Director, National Wildlife Federation executive, and then conservation writer, had become a friend. Ernie and I spent many long hours talking about conservation issues and wildlife law enforcement. He also encouraged me to take the federal exam. Sometime in the fall of '62, I did. Then I went back to work, still trying to learn something about those who use the wilderness.

Who knows when rookie days are over? Maybe never. But there comes a time in anyone's career when he or she feels it is time to move on. As much as I enjoyed my job, our friends and neighbors, and the part of the world that we were living in, I knew there were new challenges I needed to explore. Maybe that's the over-thirty syndrome. I don't know. But I could see in my work that there was a need for enforcement of the wildlife laws on an interstate and international level. I suddenly felt I should be part of that effort.

I knew I had accomplished something in my small area of jurisdiction. I had learned what I had been taught by big Ed and little Ed, that I "wasn't going to clean up the country." But I had also learned that there was a monumental job to do nationwide. I now felt I needed to be part of that effort. Therefore, I was sincere about taking the federal exam. I was ready for a new challenge.

Last laugh

In the north country, there seemed to be an attitude held by a large share of the public that was part of history. It seemed popular and fair game to brag about outwitting or outrunning the game warden. In some places, and especially in the north country, beating the game warden became more important than committing the violation.

The general public for many years seemed to take lightly those who violated fish and game laws. It was always understood that premeditating fish and game violators were considered clever or witty when they pulled one over on the game warden. Great and sometimes exaggerated tales of how I outfoxed or fooled the clumsy warden have forever been told over the bar or out in the hunting or fishing camp.

There are stories of how I just dropped the illegal fish over the side as the warden arrived, or how I slipped my deer or goose tag onto the animal just before the warden drove up. Then there are always those tales of how I hid in the brush pile or under the car or how I scampered into the barn while the warden searched in vain.

These stories and many more always brought hoots and roars of laughter from the boys at the bar. Joe's funniest story is how he hid his extra trout in his boots just as the warden walked up, and Jack's best is the time he hid his rifle beneath his wife's skirts when he was stopped by the wildlife officer. Lots of stories, some of them true, some better each time told. Some were humorous, others not so funny.

I have never been able to understand the unwritten rule of the woods that wardens are not clever when they use binoculars or telescopes to watch violators from a distance. Nor do I sympathize with those who think that it is unfair, undignified, and certainly infringing on the sportsmen's rights for a warden, not wearing a uniform, to suddenly appear from nowhere. And, of course, hiding behind trees or pretending to be another hunter or fisherman just has to be illegal. Wardens in unmarked cars have to be as sneaky as coyotes.

Even in 1963, a lot of those anti-warden attitudes were changing. Serious fish and game violators were no longer popular with the general public. More people seemed to see the fish and game as belonging to the people and not to the warden or the state or the "king." I have always believed that when violators take fish and game illegally, they are taking from their neighbors and from those hunters and fishermen who try to play by the rules.

Wildlife officers don't have to apologize for outwitting fish and game outlaws, outlaws who are dedicated to their illegal activities. I have never felt I was being underhanded or unfair when I used scientific techniques and handed-down warden tricks of the trade to catch the wildlife outlaw.

I have been outrun, outdriven, outwitted, outmaneuvered, and outwaited—fairly, unfairly, and sometimes with a vengeance. Wildlife officers owe it to the resource to use every bit of wit, every ounce of technical knowledge, and every new kind of specialized equipment available to apprehend the dogged and determined wildlife outlaw. Today this battle has moved also to the city streets and business places. But sometimes, beating the game warden can still turn out to be a game between the officer and the violator. Let me tell you about one such game I thought more fun than anything else.

I have to admit that hunters and fishermen have concocted some pretty ingenious plots to beat the game warden, even if it was just to have a good laugh. One such group of hunters I checked frequently called themselves Outlaws Incorporated. Their deer camp had those words chiseled into the marble mantle of their fireplace.

I had apprehended several of their party riding the deer trails with loaded guns and had taken them to court. They had paid their fines and given me no trouble.

This group of hunters had a big yellow van they used solely for the deer hunting season. One afternoon, I was driving along the north-woods back roads when my partner and I saw the yellow van driving slowly ahead of us. The occupants appeared to be cruising the roads looking for a standing deer, perfectly legal if their guns were unloaded and in cases.

After following the van for a short time, I said to my partner, who was new on the job, "I'm going to pull them over and check out their guns. They have a habit of riding with them loaded." I pulled up close behind the van and threw on the red light and the siren. We were soon to be surprised.

Before my partner and I could get out of our patrol car, the back door of the van flew open. Out marched eight hunters all dressed in blaze-orange. They came out just like a well-trained rifle squad. Their guns were all in cases and they were following the orders of one of the group.

"On the double, one, two, one, two. Squad halt, attention!" The men lined up in front of my car in a perfectly straight line.

"Present arms!" their drill sergeant shouted. Each hunter stripped his gun of its case and presented his gun for my inspection. I took the cue. I stepped forward to each hunter, and as I approached, the hunter slammed open the action to show me that the gun was empty.

After I had seen all guns, the drill sergeant barked out, "Pa—

rade— rest." At this point he spun around briskly and saluted. My partner looked stunned. I wanted to laugh, but I made sure I didn't crack a smile. I returned the salute and continued.

"Sergeant, have your men display their hunting licenses." At that point my partner and I approached each hunter. Each hunter stepped forward quickly, displayed his license. Each then saluted and stepped back.

After returning all licenses and salutes, I did a quick about-face and said, "Well done, men. Sergeant, dismiss your troops."

"Recase guns, for—ward—march, one, two, one, two," the sergeant barked. The nine men marched briskly into the truck, slammed the door, and roared off in a cloud of smoke—and I am sure, a truck full of side-busting laughter.

Maybe I had learned something about who uses the wilderness and who really cares, in my last eight years as a Wisconsin warden. There truly are some bad guys. And there are also some good guys. But most of the people I had met fit somewhere in between. My education, it appears, had just begun. I still remembered Spring Creek.

PART III

A NEW START,
A NEW CHALLENGE

Welcome to Minnesota?

On March 13, 1963, I became a federal agent (then called a U.S. game management agent) for the U.S. Fish and Wildlife Service. Jackie and I had driven to Fergus Falls, Minnesota in February to look at the station that was offered to us before we made up our minds.

We arrived on a Sunday afternoon. The temperature was thirty degrees below zero and the wind was blowing at about thirty miles per hour from the west. The North Dakota snert was whipping its way through us and even into the motel room we had reserved but decided not to stay in. Not even a stray dog was on the street. Nothing was open, not even a restaurant. Now at the hotel, we were shown a run-down room that must have been saved for someone they were trying to convince not to move to their town.

The two F&W Service employees I had the names of to call were not at home. We ended up getting a hot dog in a just closing bowling alley. We finally did find a motel where our door faced east, out of the wind. We couldn't even get something to warm our blood. We found the town was, at that time, a dry town. So we went to bed and woke up the next morning to increased winds, more snert, still no one home, and now time to head back to Wisconsin. Our first break—the wind was at our back.

So naturally with all this going for us, we decided to take the job. I moved in March. Jackie and the kids didn't join me until that summer when I returned from Canada, where I banded ducks for six weeks. Yes, it was a big change and a big challenge, both jobwise and family-wise. It was another one of those Bill Waggoner truths: "I wouldn't want to do it again, and I'm glad it's in my past and not my future."

The federal government made my day by assigning me a brand new car—a Studebaker Lark. After three years of attempting to per-form my duties in the Stupidbaker, I shed tears of thanks and joy when the Studebaker company went out of business and the government was forced to buy another make car for their agents. This book would not be complete without at least one episode involving the Lark. It is fair to tell you now, I can remember no good feelings for this machine that pretended to be an automobile.

Second gear

In the beginning, I had an immediate dislike for the Stupidbaker. Its short wheel base broke my back. It didn't like to start in cold or hot weather. Its transmission must have missed getting some of the vital ingredients that make cars go both ways—forward and reverse. After backing four miles out of a marsh road one night, because I couldn't get out of reverse, my friendly mechanic said my future didn't look good.

I was soon to learn how dependent federal agents were on their government car. I was soon to learn what the word *travel* meant. Off I went on the road to the Dakotas, Missouri, Iowa, Illinois, Michigan, and the Horicon marsh of Wisconsin. I even worked now and then in Minnesota. My phone would ring as I was unpacking my dirty clothes and introducing myself to my wife and children, and a voice would say, "What are you doing?" I would tell my new supervisor that I was just unpacking from the last assignment. He'd say something like, "How would you like to go to Missouri?" And away I would go again.

Now I was headed just over the border to North Dakota to work their early teal season. As everyone knows, you can see out across the Dakota prairies forever. There is no place to hide a car out there. I needed to hide my Lark near the road that bordered some waterfowl holding potholes. The local state officer had good information from the landowner that certain hunters would roar up, shoot anything that was alive from their car window, and disappear in a cloud of dust. The farmer said I could hide the Lark in his barn.

I parked in the barn. Sure enough, a car came down the road in an hour's time. A gun poked out the rear window and a closed-season mallard slumped its head into the water. A young man jumped out, picked up the duck, and dashed back into the car. The car roared off toward the next pothole. I threw open the barn door, rammed the Lark into gear, and roared after the illegal duck hunters.

I could see them way down the road stop at another pothole. I couldn't get the Stupidbaker out of second gear. When I got up to fifty miles per hour, I was sure either the car or I was going to blow up. I could see the culprits now leaving the second pothole. They didn't even know I was chasing them. I continued after the disappearing car, saying unkind words to my stuttering, jerky, forty-mile-per-hour friend. Both the Stupidbaker and I were smoking inside.

As far as I know, the illegal road hunters are still going. I never did get close enough to even identify them.

After three years of bad times and three transmissions, I said goodbye to the Stupidbaker. By then I knew what the astronauts meant when they said, "Our confidence is 'high,' knowing that all our equipment has been purchased through the GSA [General Services Administration], on the lowest bid."

The black angus strikes again

During my early days as a federal agent, I had little time to scout my new territory around Fergus Falls because I was away so much. I am not sure I knew where all the rooms were in our newly rented house. But I did get to know several local state wardens who *did* know the country. When the waterfowl season opened in my area, I teamed up with Jim Meyers from Elbow Lake; I liked Jim immediately.

Jim directed me in my car to Lake Christina, a western Minnesota lake famous for canvasbacks. We had just put my boat into the lake with about thirty minutes until shooting hours. We were just climbing in, along with my old deputy Midnight, when we heard BOOM! BOOM! from not far down the lake. It sounded like the shots came from about a half mile into the lower lake. We hadn't planned on checking hunters on that bay now, but it sounded like we ought to.

We could get to the shooting by running our boat through the culvert. We had everything ready to go. So we churned through the culvert and headed toward the point where we heard the early shooting. We had taken Midnight along just in case we needed to look for ducks. (For some reason Midnight always liked to ride on the front seat at the very tip of the bow of the boat. He looked like a giant hood ornament as he stood pointing into the wind.)

Just as we came within a hundred yards or so of the point of land where we figured the shooting came from, we saw two hunters. One was in the blind. The other was wading back toward the big blind. The second hunter might have been carrying something. We gunned our boat toward the men.

When we arrived at their straw-bail blind, both hunters were sitting having a cup of coffee. They both looked very relaxed. It was still fifteen minutes until the legal shooting hour. These two hunters sure seemed to be in the right location to have done the early shooting, but they were doing everything now to look like they were not the guilty parties.

As we hit the bank, Midnight bounded out onto the dry land. His nose was working into the wind. We asked the two hunters if they had heard the early shooting. They said they had, but didn't know where it came from. "Probably farther up the lake," one of the men replied.

We asked to see their licenses and stamps, and then checked their gun plugs. I noticed that the barrel on the gun I checked was just a little warm.

Midnight had made a loop and was on to something. He twirled his tail right up to a big oak, stopped, dove in, and came out with a big red-legged mallard. It was still steaming. My hunter had been watching the big dog out of the corner of his eye. He almost jumped when he saw the dog grab the duck.

Midnight came straight on a beeline to my hunter. He went right to his feet and laid down the mallard, pretty as a painting. "Go away, dog," the man said, as much as to say, "That's not my duck."

But Midnight wasn't satisfied. The big dog wheeled around and dashed straight back to the big oak. He came again right to the hunter I was checking. This time he sat with a second mallard in his mouth. His tail wagged like crazy. The hunter looked at the dog, then looked at his partner, as much as to say, "What the hell do I say now?" Then he looked at me and shrugged his shoulders. I noticed a little blood on his hands.

Jim and I wrote the man up for possession of two mallards during the closed season. The hunter decided to give us a statement. We decided not to charge him with shooting before hours. Midnight was proud of his retrieves, all three of them.

Foot in mouth

One of the Indian reservations in northern Minnesota was the site of a continual waterfowl overbagging problem for us. It wasn't the Indians, in this case, that were shooting too many ducks. Instead, a few white men would hire an Indian guide, as required, and proceed to slaughter all the diving ducks they could blast out of the sky.

One Saturday morning, one of the state officers and I got ourselves into a good location, where we could observe three or four hunting parties. Gordy had brought along his big Chesapeake, named Charger. Charger was exactly that. He was big and strong and an excellent retriever. Gordy claimed Charger could smell a duck buried under ten feet of spaghetti sauce.

Gordy and I watched these two hunters shoot and shoot. We had been able to mark down the time of almost every drop since our arrival, but we felt strongly that they had over their bag of birds. We decided we should move in and check them out. When we approached the two hunters, they immediately became obnoxious.

"Hurry up and check our ducks and get on your way. We're paying a guide ten dollars a day and we want to get our money's worth."

The Indian guide was sitting back on a stump. He had a bottle and wasn't in good guiding shape. Most of the guides that worked the reservation were good. This guy wasn't of the same quality. The hunters had just eight bluebills in their possession. They claimed four of the eight were the guide's birds. He had a license. The limit was four apiece, so these wise guys still had four to go.

We were just about ready to back our boat out when Charger, who had been roaming around the hunter's blind, stopped almost at the blind. He went close to the hunter's feet and started to dig. The most obnoxious hunter really got angry now. He kicked at the dog and shouted.

"Get the hell out of here, you big overgrown mongrel."

Gordy and I started back out of our boat, fed up with this guy's abuse. But before we could say anything, Charger grabbed onto the kicking foot *very firmly*. The hunter yowled. Gordy called Charger off, and the dog went right back to his digging.

Now I could see a feather, or was it a wing? It was a wing. It was a duck. Charger kept digging. Gordy went over to make sure there was no more interference from our unfriendly hunter. I helped Charger dig.

There were thirteen more ducks in the hole. They were all freshly killed. We checked each one with a thermometer. Duck temperatures just at death are about 107°F. They will gradually lose this temperature at a fairly constant rate, depending to some degree on the weather and how the duck is kept. These birds were all in the 90°–101° range. They had all been killed in the last several hours.

We cited the two noisy hunters into court. The guide later gave us a statement about the activities of his patrons. I think he was encouraged to cooperate by some of the better guides on the lake. They didn't go along with the antics of these two.

In court, the dog kicker began to complain about the dog grabbing him by the foot.

"Mr. Padlock, I think if you decided to kick me I might want to bite you too," the judge remarked. "You are fortunate that the warden was there to stop the dog. I've seen Charger. He probably could have made a real impression on you, had he been allowed to. I'm going to fine you the maximum and restrict you from hunting on the reservation for three years. And for taking thirteen ducks over the limit, I'm going to fine you twenty dollars a duck. People like you two give the reservation a bad name. Next case."

Calling card caper

There are two kinds of duck hunting clubs. The club can be well run with strict safety rules and rules of conduct that are adhered to without exception by the members, or you're out; or a club can become a nest of bandits or sophisticated violators, who care little for any code of conduct or regulations.

An old-time local duck hunter finally became fed up with the gross violations he knew about at the Elbow Bend duck club near my western Minnesota agent station. The old-timer told me that club had just about driven out all the good duck hunters from the area. The local hunters had put up with the violations and unsportsmanlike conduct for years. They had finally decided that the ducks and the sport were really theirs and not the state's or the federal government's—and not exclusively the Elbow Bend's.

It took two years to get enough information to effectively work the Elbow Bend club. In cooperation with the state wardens, two other agents and I set up on the club early one fall morning.

Having scouted the area during the previous summer, we knew where buildings were located, where the pass shooting pits were located, and how hunters could get from the club buildings to hunting areas on foot and by vehicle.

At 5 A.M., two of us were in position to watch "the pass" and the hunters on the pass. Basically there were four hunters that came to hunt this particular area of the club. Diving ducks swarmed between the two parts of Elbow Bend Lake all day, providing shooting that most hunters just dream about. We were watching from two different locations.

We clocked every shot and recorded every duck down, by which hunter, all day long. We gradually learned that White Coat was the real killer of the group. When he raised his gun, ducks came down. The other hunters killed ducks on and off during the day. The fourth hunter shot, but never hit birds. He was, however, the official or unofficial duck retriever, the one who hid the birds.

As the day grew on, we developed names for each hunter. There was Shorty, dressed in a brown coat, brown hat, and hip boots. Fat Stuff wore a black and red checked coat and always had a cigar protruding from his mouth. Then there was Glasses, the guy who retrieved all the birds. He hid them under trees, in roots, and in the branches of trees. Lastly there was White Coat. He shot over five boxes of shells from 6 A.M. until about 5 P.M., in between beer breaks. All the hunters participated in the beer breaks. When the day's shooting came to a halt due to darkness, we counted sixty-seven divers that had been dropped on the pass.

I was lying down near the pass, hiding behind a big tree at the edge of a marsh off to the side of the pass. I was close enough to hear comments and remarks made by the hunters. Agent Orton was up on a hill, looking right down the hunters' throats with his 30-power scope. He was recording every shot fired. We had portable radios and maintained radio contact with each other and another agent in his car, who was standing by with a state officer for the final bust.

We had mapped the location of all the ducks hidden by Glasses during the day. Agent Orton called me at about 4 P.M.

"White Coat has left the pit and is walking toward you with his Irish Setter. He is carrying eight ducks."

While White Coat strode toward me, I rolled carefully away from the tree and down into the mud and the water and the cover of the marsh grass. White Coat walked up to the big tree, reached around without looking behind it, and hung the eight ducks (a two-day limit) on a nail on my side of the tree. Then he and the dog walked back to the pit blind and continued to shoot more ducks.

It was time to move in. The hunters were getting ready to quit hunting for the day. They had shot over 1½ cases of shells. (After White Coat had hung his ducks on the nail on the back of the tree, I had crawled back to the tree and inserted one of my calling cards down the throat of one of the bluebills.)

Using our radios, we all moved in at the same time. Our car came in through the locked gate with the aid of a bolt cutter. I walked over and met Glasses as he was putting his gun away in a little ammo house near the pass. I broke the news to him by identifying myself with my credentials.

"I didn't shoot a duck all day long."

"I know, but I am going to ask you to go and get all the birds you hid in the trees and roots. We have each bird mapped and each shot recorded."

Glasses wanted to tell me more, but I told him to just show me his license, stamp, and gun. I didn't want any statements; I had been here watching him for thirteen hours. I had recorded each time he drank a beer and each time he went to the bathroom. I could see tears in his eyes. We soon had "all" the ducks in a pile, the duck hunters together, and all the guns stacked up on the hood of state warden O'Brien's car. But not all the ducks.

"Is that all the ducks?" I asked the hunters.

"Yes," they all answered together.

"Mr. Huwiter, are you aware of any more birds you might have forgotten?" I asked White Coat. "You said you wanted to cooperate." Again, White Coat said that's all he knew of.

"Come on with me," I said. We walked to the big tree. I reached around the tree and removed the eight ducks, without looking, just as he had done when he placed them there. I carried them back to the group.

"Mr. Huwiter, have you seen these eight ducks before?" I asked once more.

"Not those ducks."

I reached down into the throat of one of the bluebills and pulled out my calling card. I unrolled it and read what I had written there an hour before: "White Coat with Irish Setter—eight bluebills on nail— 4:08 P.M." It was signed by me.

The four hunters were prominent businessmen from Minneapolis. They hired a high-priced attorney and fought their case. They lost. They also paid $250 apiece and lost their Browning automatics. For a while, at least, the local hunters went back to hunting the area around Elbow Bend Lake. These four hunters knew they were wrong.

Instant mallard

Some people, when they go hunting or fishing, get carried away with the unusual success or spirit of the group and bag way over the limit of waterfowl. I'd like to tell you about a hunter who had only one thought on his mind when he went hunting—to kill every bird he could, in any way he could.

Weiner, Arkansas, along with Stutgart and several other southern mallard paradises, was in need of some concentrated waterfowl enforcement effort. About forty federal agents were detailed into the area to team up with state officers. We were told overbagging was quite common in these red-hot mallard hunting areas. The forty agents represented about one fourth of the agents in the nation in the 1960s. There aren't many more today.

For three or four days, we patrolled the area rice field, but could hardly find a duck or a duck hunter to check. On Friday night some weather moved in. It clouded up, cooled off, and all the mallards in the world came to Arkansas. I had never seen mallards like that before in my life. Take a blue sky full of nothing, add a little weather, and you've got instant mallard.

After making several overbag cases, my state officer partner and I were resting, parked along a road, watching about 500 mallards swarm into a rice field about three-quarters of a mile south of us. There was a pickup truck parked about two miles east of us, but anyone hunting around the truck was too far away to get a crack at these vulnerable, circling birds.

Just as I started to pour some coffee, my partner stopped me. He pointed out across the field toward the truck. I got out my field glasses and scanned the area around the ducks. There was a crawling hunter. He was moving slowly and carefully toward the swarming ducks.

Each time the big flock of mallards swung around, they would pass over the hunter. He would duck down and not even raise his gun. He apparently wasn't going to be satisfied with trying to pick off a couple of the stragglers and go home with his two-duck limit. He had bigger goals on his mind.

I put away my coffee cup and grabbed my cane. For years, I would carry a cane in the field to look like a gun when I approached hunters. It made me look like one of the boys until I got close enough to become someone else. I was far enough away that the crawling hunter would probably not even see me start toward the field, even if he was watching. I ran to the drainage ditch, which was deep enough and dry enough for me to run in a squatted position and still be concealed. I headed for the swarming mallards, just as my crawling friend on the other end of the field had.

After I had run 200 yards, I stopped and peered up over the ditch. I could see the mallards were just about satisfied with the appearance of the rice field. They were starting to settle onto the ground. I was now about seventy yards away. At first I didn't see my crawling hunter. Then I did. Now he was up; just as the mallards settled to the ground, he had jumped to his feet. He fired three times into the flock.

I could see crippled ducks flopping in all directions. The hunter ran to the mallards and started hitting the cripples on the head with his gun barrel. When he turned his back to grab several birds for his pile, I leaped up and ran full speed toward the hunter. I got within about thirty yards when the hunter stopped. Then he spun around to look right at me. I knew he didn't hear me. He could just feel I was coming.

"Hold it right there, don't move." He didn't even breathe. I reached him, identified myself, took his gun, and told him to keep catching birds until we got all the cripples we could. I put several out of their misery with my cane. When we finished, we had twenty-two mallards lying in a pile on the ground before us. Several had flown weakly away.

"Let's go back to the car," I said, after taking down all the information I needed from the hunter. "The state officer is there waiting for us. Pick up your gun." I hung the twenty-two mallards, which were all thrown in a gunnysack by my hunter (it just happened to be on his belt), over his gun barrel.

"You shot them, you carry them," I said.

Twenty-two mallards, Arkansas mallards, weigh about sixty pounds. By the time my thirty-year-old hunter made it to our car, he had worked up quite a sweat for such a cool day. The state officer wasn't surprised to see who I had apprehended. This was the third time this young man had been arrested for ground-swatting ducks in the rice fields.

I heard later that the hunter paid a $200 fine and lost his license for one year. He went to state court. I don't know if he learned anything from the experience. But I learned that day that a man can kill twenty-two or more mallards with three shots, if he knows how to do it. His gun would only hold three shots. I have often wondered how many ducks he would have killed had he used an unplugged, six-shot automatic shotgun.

Warmed up for the judge

Both state and federal wildlife officers know that waterfowl populations suffer from double trippers. Double trippers are hunters who kill their limit of ducks or geese, hustle them off to some hiding place (often the home freezer), and then return to the marsh for their second limit.

Double trippers are hard to apprehend. An officer must observe the taking of the first limit, know where the ducks or geese are cached, and then observe and apprehend this greedy hunter with the second-bag limit. The wildlife officer must do all this without the greedy hunter suspecting he is being observed.

Special agents of the U.S. Fish and Wildlife Service have the authority to work anywhere in the United States. They are often assigned to some far-off state to help other agents with special problems. As a Minnesota agent, I found myself heading off for weeks on end to the Dakotas, Illinois, Iowa, or Missouri. This made for a long, cold duck season. (My wife spent many a night waiting for these seasons to be over.)

I arrived late one fall in Missouri (where everyone waves at everyone else as they drive by) to find that double tripping was a really serious problem. Wayne Sanders, the agent-in-charge of the state, felt local wardens and agents were soon recognized by the habitual double trippers.

"Try to melt in with the other hunters and maybe you can latch on to one of them doing his overbag thing," he said. Wayne knew his county. "Head down in your unmarked government Studebaker Lark. There are some cornfields near Murphysville where I know overbaggers and double trippers are killing a lot of ducks."

It was an early December morning when I parked the Stupidbaker alongside some grain storage bins, among other hunters' cars across from some partially harvested cornfields. The fields were filled with hunters. I arranged the contents of my car, putting my radio microphone under the seat to make it look as much like another hunter's car as possible.

You don't wear a uniform and wave a resource flag when you're trying to apprehend a premeditating double tripper in the act. There is a time for a wildlife officer to wear a uniform and there is a time *not* to wear a uniform. This was one of those times when you shouldn't.

Unfortunately, there are some people in the non-enforcement wildlife department hierarchy who don't understand this basic enforcement and human nature truth. This is how "always in uniform" rules sometimes prevent wildlife officers from apprehending the real outlaws.

Fortunately, I operated under no such federal guidelines on this cold, snow-filled morning.

I pulled on my down vest, hunting coat, heavy gloves, and grabbed my old 20-gauge shotgun for effect. A man walking out into a field full of waterfowl hunters without a shotgun sticks out like a bald woman in a crowded beauty shop. It was snowing hard as I locked the Lark and started toward the hunting field.

Most hunters were already in place in field blinds built out of snow fence and camouflaged with cornstalks piled alongside. The birds were flying. As only longtime winter duck hunters know, when the snow comes down and the wind starts moving it in a horizontal direction, get ready. The ducks fly almost on the ground. Shooting is good for those who can tough out these weather conditions.

I was cold already as I crawled into an old blind and pulled out my binoculars and notebook. Checking waterfowl hunters is a painstaking and tedious ordeal. An officer must identify each hunter in his circle of observation. He must chart who fires each shot and who retrieves each bird. He must also keep foolproof records as to when everything happens. It can be a cold, exacting business. This kind of hunter checking is patience-stretching, and it is the reason some wildlife officers won't work waterfowl hunters.

I stayed in the field for several hours until my hands started to turn as white as the day and my nose as blue as my car. It wasn't a day to bounce from blind to blind checking licenses, duck stamps, and gun plugs. Instead it was a day to wait and observe.

I was there to work overbaggers and double trippers. Once I tipped my hand and started routinely checking hunters at their blinds, overbagging and double tripping would be over (in that locality) for the day. Those prone to cheat on limits—and that includes an awful lot of hunters under certain circumstances—do so much more readily when they feel their party is alone and unobserved.

The snow was coming down now as if out of a wind tunnel. I couldn't see the hunters or the ducks. Shooting was letting up. I felt as effective as a blind man trying to count blackbirds on a telephone wire by listening for the sounds they make. I needed a cup of coffee.

I headed for the Lark. I stomped my feet in the snow as I hurried back toward the few cars left. I fumbled for my keys, got in, and started up the car. Soon I had the heater going. It wasn't long before I could feel myself coming back to life. My hands started to ache; I knew my circulation was beginning again. The hot coffee from my thermos helped me believe I was going to survive. I had been gone a week and I decided it would be a good time to write my wife a letter.

I had started Dear Jackie, and was about halfway to Love, Dave, when I saw a snowman trudging toward me. This snowman was carrying a shotgun and two big, fat mallards—his limit for the day. He came right up to the car parked next to mine. He tossed the ducks onto the ground and fumbled with his car door. He finally got in and got his engine running. He looked frozen.

I rolled down the window and asked, "How did you do?" His car door was still open. He got out and came over.

"I got my two. Say, would you mind if I sit in with you until my car warms up? I'm frozen."

"Not at all. Come on, get in."

He shook off the snow and climbed into the warm interior of Uncle Sam's Lark. My guest soon thawed out enough to talk. He asked about my Minnesota license plate and what I was doing in Missouri. I told him I had business in the nearby town and took some time out to take in a little duck hunting. He asked me if I had any luck, meaning ducks. I told him no, meaning duck hunters.

Once my guest had assured himself I was not a warden, but instead another cold hunter like himself, he began to tell me about his hunting successes. He told me how he hunted almost every day. He told me how he had filled his freezer with ducks at home. (Legal possession limit was twice the daily bag limit.) Except for those birds he could claim belonged to family members, all the rest he had in his freezer were illegal.

"Are you going out again?" the thawed-out hunter asked me. "The ducks are really swarming into the field now."

"No, I've had about all the snow and cold I can take for one day. When I finish this letter I guess I'll be heading back toward town."

His car now warmed, my guest thanked me and climbed into his own vehicle. I looked around the car. I was glad I had tidied up my interior; warden charts, lawbooks, radios and binoculars are sure giveaways.

My friend appeared to be warming up to go out again. Why else would he not now be on his way home? The swarming ducks were just too much for him. I figured I would give the man a chance to do what he had probably done for years: double trip.

I left. I waved as I backed out around the corncrib and other cars. I headed down the road toward town. I stopped just over the first hill, grabbed my binoculars and heavy coat, and walked back to where I could see the corncrib and the car belonging to my "new friend" George.

As I suspected, within fifteen minutes of more snow and freezing cold, I saw George cross the road, gun in hand, heading for the circling mallards. I heard lots of shooting after George got back to his blind. But because of the blinding snow, I couldn't see what success he had. I knew he had his limit at the car. One more was too much.

About an hour later, so cold I was beginning to shake, I stomped back to my car and drove back to the corncrib parking lot. I timed my arrival just as George opened the trunk of his car and tossed in two steaming mallards. As I walked up to him, he looked a little puzzled to see me.

"Decided to go back after the ducks?" I asked.

"Yeh, you too?"

"No, George, I decided to stay around and see if you might brave the cold for a goose, or if you might really go back and kill more mallards for your freezer. The full freezer you were telling me about."

I pulled out my credentials with my numbed hands and identified myself as a federal agent. I asked George if he would get out the two mallards he had killed earlier. He just shrugged his shoulders, but didn't move. It had stopped snowing and I could make out snowed-over tracks around George's car. I could see that he was not going to produce the overlimit of mallards without assistance.

"George, why don't you get me the extra birds. It will make it much easier for both of us. You didn't rob the First National Bank, and I'm not going to treat you like you did."

George still didn't move. He acted as if he knew something I didn't. I suspected now the first mallards would not be so easy to find. They were probably hidden somewhere in his car.

I could arrest George and search his car, but I preferred not to. I would rather, as was our usual procedure, write George a violation notice or just tell him he would be receiving one in the mail. The violation notice gave him the choice of paying by mail or going to court.

But George was not budging. Maybe his surprise at seeing me again, finding out I was a federal agent, and his second freezing trip out into the elements had combined to make him inadvertently uncooperative.

I looked around for signs of the extra mallards. I could see some faint, snowed-on man-tracks leading from George's car in the direction of the corncrib. I asked George to take the freshly killed mallards out of the trunk and hand them to me. He did. I asked him to stay where he was until I explored the tracks in the snow.

I could see the tracks better as I got to the back of the corncrib, out of the wind. They appeared to be George-sized bootprints coming and going at the crib. Under the crib, I could see the snow was mussed. I called out to George, fifty feet away.

"Come over here, Mr. Karney." He came. "Do you remember putting anything under this crib this morning?"

"I'll get the ducks. I put them there after you left."

I took down all the information I needed on George and gave him a violation notice. The notice would require him to send a court-scheduled fine to the judge, or he could request a hearing.

After leaving George and taking the four mallards with me, I called the local state officer and told him he should put a surveillance on George's house. I also said I would be along shortly to provide testimony for obtaining a search warrant for the freezer full of ducks that George bragged about.

Before we could obtain the warrant, George obliged us by hurrying home and loading six boxes of mallards into his car, bound for his brother's freezer. The state officer, watching his house, arrested him on the spot and hauled George off to jail.

George paid a fine in federal court for overbagging (double tripping). He also paid a healthy fine in state court and lost his hunting privileges for one year, for having in his possession sixty-three mallards. He also spent several hours in jail.

Some people might wonder why a federal agent stationed in Minnesota, a member of one of the smallest federal enforcement agencies in the nation, would travel all the way to Missouri just to apprehend a double tripper. But can you think of a better way to get George's attention? It could just possibly change his overbagging tendencies. It also might set an example, for George's friends and other hunters. We wildlife officers can dream, can't we?

I like to think back on all the questions that George asked me when he was warming up in Uncle Sam's patrol vehicle. Of all the questions he asked, trying to feel out if I might be a game warden, he didn't ask me if I was one. I would have told him. Instead, he warmed himself over the government heater for a trip to see the judge.

"The boy did it!"

When some people are caught violating a fish or game law, they verbally attack everyone within range. If I hadn't been there, I wouldn't believe this story.

A lot of people have heard of the huge population of Canada geese that swarm into the Horicon marsh in central Wisconsin each fall. Hundreds of thousands of the big birds pile into a tiny ten-mile or so area, in and around the state and national wildlife refuges.

While on assignment there one fall, another agent and I observed a car stop and a gun being stuck out the back window. We heard a shotgun blast and saw a goose drop next to the road, as the rest of the flock flew off. We pulled out of our secluded observation point and, with red light flashing, took off in pursuit of the shooter's car. At first slow to respond to the red light and the siren, the car finally stopped alongside the heavily traveled highway.

As we approached the shooter's car on foot, it began to rain. As I approached the rear door along the road ditch side, I saw a young boy, about sixteen years old, trying feverishly to lock a required goose tag around the leg of a still-kicking goose. I identified myself by showing my credentials.

"Step out and hand me the goose."

He did. It was untagged. The rest of the boy's family—mother, younger sister, and father (at the wheel)—didn't say anything at the time. The rain started to come down harder.

"Come back to my car, please," I said to the boy and his father. "I want to discuss this situation with you both." They climbed into the back seat of my car, out of the rain. I had locked the goose in the trunk. I turned around in the seat so that I could talk to the man and his son. I told the father that I wanted to see some identification.

"I don't know why you want to see my idemnification." Pointing to the boy, he said, "He shot the goose."

"Please get out your identification, sir."

The rain started to come down in torrents; it seemed the weatherman was involved in making our situation more tense. The man now started to get quite red in the face. He pulled out his billfold and started to pull cards and licenses out and slap them down on the back of the seat between us. I could see he was getting out everything from a driver's license to an Elks Club card. He had cards stretched all along the top of the seat. Starting to sweat profusely, he raised his voice to a high pitch.

"There, now you see all my idemnification. Now I want to see *your* idemnification."

I pulled out my credentials again and turned them toward the quite excited man in the back seat. I started to explain that I had shown them to him and the boy when I first confronted them, but before I could explain, the sweating man snatched the credentials from my hand.

"Now I've got your idemnification," he bellowed.

At that point I looked into the man's eyes; they were wild. The rain continued to come down harder. The windows started to steam up. I'm sure my partner saw the same wildness in the man's eyes that

I did, but the confines of the car and the uncomfortable positions we were sitting in made just talking difficult.

I pulled out a calling card and handed it to the excited man.

"Please hand back the credentials after you look them over. Take this card. It has all the information you need on it as to my identity."

The boy sat unmoving, apparently scared to death. After nervously opening and closing and rubbing and examining the credentials, the nervous man hesitantly reached forward with them and snatched the card. I took the credentials carefully. At least we weren't out on some lake where people have grabbed officers' credentials and thrown them overboard.

I could see the man was a little calmer.

"You understand, Mr. Stukowski, that I am concerned with your part in the taking of this goose from the window of your car. Your boy here could not have shot the goose or picked it up if you, the driver, and his father, had not allowed him to do it. That makes you an accessory to the crime."

This statement put Mr. Stukowski right into orbit. His face turned beet-red, his brow dripped with sweat, and his knuckles were white as he gripped the seat between us. His voice became very high pitched.

"The boy did it! He killed the goose!"

The boy pulled back into the corner. I could see the circumstances would not allow a quiet discussion with Mr. Stukowski.

"You and I are going to take a walk in the rain. Unless you are able to calm yourself down, I will be forced to place you under arrest and take you in to the sheriff's office."

With that, I jumped out of the car, went around to Stukowski's side of the car near the road ditch, and opened his door. When I got the door opened, I found myself looking into the eyes of a man near panic. I took him gently by the arm and helped him out into the driving rain. We walked out into an open field away from the highway and the traffic. We walked fast. We were soaked in just a few minutes. When we were both sopped and puffing from the brisk pace, I stopped and pulled Stukowski around to face me.

"Now, Mr. Stukowski, are you calm enough to discuss this problem, or must I put cuffs on you and take you to jail? I don't want to do that to you in front of your family, but you're giving me no choice."

I pulled out the cuffs and waited for his reply. Suddenly, almost as quickly as his wild-eyed appearance had come, it disappeared. The rain and the open field, away from the confines of the car, had done the job.

With the rain streaming down his nose, he suddenly dropped his arms to his sides. I could see he had wilted. He was ready to come back to my car and listen to what would happen next.

Once back in the car, I had my partner get in the back seat with the boy, and got Stukowski in the front with me. The wet and subdued man listened to me explain our ticketing system.

"I am charging you with shooting a Canada goose from a motor vehicle and failing to tag the goose before transporting it, as required by law."

I gave him a violation notice and told him if he in any way took out his frustrations on the boy, he would face charges much more severe than the misdemeanor charges he now faced for the illegal goose. Once I was convinced that the man was calm enough to drive, I took him and the boy back to his car and told him I would see him in court the following week. I wasn't letting him handle this through the mail as ordinarily I might.

Stukowski came to court with his wife. The magistrate read the two charges to him. He asked Stukowski how he pleaded to the charges. Before the meek man could answer, his wife did.

"He pleads guilty to both charges." And when asked by the judge if he had anything to say before sentencing, Mrs. Stukowski replied, "He has nothing to say." He paid the fine.

A month later, Mr. Stukowski wrote to his congressman, complaining about how he was charged with a crime someone else had committed. I didn't hear any more about the case after I reported through channels to the congressman. I explained, as best I could, how a man could aid and abet in the killing of a goose and then turn on his own son and say, "The boy did it!"

The wrong tree

As a new federal agent, I was sent each of the six years I was stationed in Fergus Falls, Minnesota, to the Horicon marsh for the fall goose season. When as many as 200,000 Canada geese congregate in an area less than ten miles in circumference, almost anything can happen. Add in the ingredients of unharvested corn, rain, unhappy farmers, over-enthusiastic hunters, goose quota systems concerning many states, and tight restrictions on the hunting of the geese, and the Horicon marsh area can become a pretty wild place. And all the wild animals aren't geese.

Some wildlife violators are so smart that they outsmart themselves.

The "wrong-tree" goose hunters had played their little game before. Another agent and I were patrolling some field just a few miles from the Horicon National Wildlife Refuge.

"My gosh, look at the geese!" my partner said.

As we turned a corner, we were looking out onto a just harvested cornfield. The harvesting had left a great deal of scattered corn in the field. There were enough Canada geese feeding in that field to fill a hundred boxcars. The hunting season was open. But the quota system allowed hunters, under permit, to kill one goose per hunter, per season. And a locking metal tag had to be locked to the goose immediately after taking. The geese in this field seemed to care not at all that they were feeding within a stone's throw of the gravel road. A hunter could almost kill a goose with a baseball bat.

My partner and I stopped the car and glassed the field. On the far end next to the road, a small car was parked within only fifty feet or so from the vulnerable geese. I thought I saw a gun being pulled into the car as we pulled up on top of the hill. My car had no markings on it to indicate we were enforcement officers.

I decided to drive on by the small car. There were two men in the car. They were dressed as hunters. I drove over the first rise in the road.

"Grab your radio and binoculars," I said to my young partner, "and drop off here in the woods. I'll pull over the hill and get out of the way. You climb behind a tree and let's allow our hunter friends to do whatever they decide they want to do."

Bob jumped out. I drove over the hill and rolled down an old field road that led down into another cornfield. As soon as I parked, Bob called on the radio. He said the little car had left the field, but a station wagon had arrived and the hunters in the wagon were really looking over the geese. Bob suggested he stay where he was behind the tree.

"Good idea, let's see what these new hunters are up to."

I almost swallowed my pipe when Bob called back and told me what was happening back in the woods.

"The station wagon pulled past the geese and drove right up to the same little woods where I'm hidden," he whispered. "Two men have now gotten out. They have walked to the back of the wagon." Bob's voice became very low. "They are only twenty feet from me now. I'll call again when they aren't so close." I waited a few minutes and then heard Bob's excited voice again.

"I can't believe this. The two guys pulled ten geese out of the wagon's trunk compartment and threw them behind the nearest tree. Then they shut the tailgate, got back in the wagon and drove back to the cornfield. Now there are four hunters from the wagon out in the field stalking the geese.''

"Sounds like you have a grandstand seat for the rest of the play, Bob. Keep me informed. I'll stay where I am and come when you call.''

Bob watched as the four hunters crawled up on the feeding geese and managed to shoot and retrieve five more geese. Meanwhile, Bob had checked out and counted the geese behind the tree. There *were* ten, and they were all untagged. The four hunters now had fifteen birds. Not a bad shoot for four hunters when the limit was one apiece. (A permit was also required for each bird.)

Needless to say, there were four surprised hunters when they returned to the woods and started to reload their first ten geese.

"Hello there, I'm a federal agent,'' Bob said as he stepped from behind the tree. I drove up at exactly the same moment.

During the investigation and prosecution that followed, I became convinced that these hunters had played their game of hide and seek before, probably each time they went goose hunting. Stashing the geese in the woods behind a tree had always worked before. This time they chose the wrong tree. It was the only tree in the county that had a federal agent behind it.

The perfect sneak

Wild animals often do foolish and crazy things. People in the outdoors do crazy things and make fools of themselves too. Oh yes, that includes wildlife officers, and unfortunately that includes me. I've seen some pretty unusual human conduct just about everywhere I have followed hunters and fishermen. But it seems where geese concentrate, hunters naturally concentrate too.

While watching some goose hunters near the Horicon marsh in Wisconsin one day, I saw a car stop alongside the road. I was on a high hill looking down on two goose hunters who had set out about twenty goose decoys in the field in front of them. They crouched in the brushy fencerow about thirty yards from the decoys.

A lone hunter got out of the car that had just arrived. The hunter hurriedly started off toward the two hunters in the fencerow. What I couldn't understand was that the newly arrived hunter began to crawl and sneak directly toward the two hunters, who waited patiently for some geese to come in to their decoys.

After the crawling hunter got almost to the fencerow, it suddenly dawned on me what he was up to. He was sneaking on the decoys. He didn't see the other hunters and thought the decoys were geese. Chuckling to myself, I wondered how the other hunters would react when the sneaker jumped up and blasted into their unpalatable decoys. The tired crawler now reached the fencerow just twenty yards from the decoys and about twenty yards from the decoy owners. Suddenly the sneak leaped to his feet, his shotgun aimed at the decoys.

I waited for the boom. There was none. At the last second, just as he was about to pull his trigger, he must have realized the motionless geese weren't geese at all. Then I saw the surprised decoy owners jump up. I could hear voices.

When the sweating decoy hunter returned to his car I was there, not to rub it in, just to find out the rest of the story. I asked the young man to show me his license and goose permit. I didn't tell him I had been watching his perfect sneak on the decoys. He showed me a hunting license, but said he didn't have a goose permit. He quickly added that he didn't shoot at any geese anyway because they got up and flew away before he got to them.

"Those geese got up and flew away before you fired a shot, did they?"

"They sure did. You can check the barrel of my gun to see I haven't fired it all day."

"That won't be necessary, young fellow. You don't need a goose permit to hunt decoys."

I walked off to check out the other two hunters on the fencerow. The young man climbed sheepishly into his car and drove off.

When I reached the decoy owners they were still laughing. They started to tell me about the guy who did a perfect sneak on their decoys. I told them I had witnessed the whole affair and related to them the part about the decoys getting up and flying away. They couldn't stop laughing.

"What did you guys say to the young fellow when he jumped up to shoot at the decoys?" I asked. The older of the two hunters replied.

"I shouted at him, 'You shoot 'em, you eat 'em.' "

From the prairies to the ocean

Jackie and I had always lived in the Midwest. Since 1963, when I first became a federal agent, I had learned a lot about waterfowl, which were the prime concern of federal agents in those days.

My last six years of duck and goose education had included enforcement assignments all over the Midwest, and in Arkansas, Louisiana, and all along the Canadian border from North Dakota to Upper Michigan. Some of my non-enforcement duties included banding mallards, pintails, teal, and other waterfowl each summer in Canada for periods of six weeks or more.

I worked on drive crews, catching and banding ducks when the mature birds were flightless in their early summer molting stage and the young were still too young to fly. I ran cannon net crews near Moosejaw, Regina, and Saskatoon, where we put in eighteen-hour days, getting to bed by nine or ten at night and up at two or three, to touch off our cannons before dawn. We had to capture our baited-in quarry before they were startled by the dawn and flew off into the sunrise.

My last eight years as a federal agent had taught me that wildlife situations and problems vary a great deal from state to state and from topography to topography. I also found each new habitat somewhat different from the last, and people's attitudes somewhat different, but in many ways the same. But always I found a need for wildlife law enforcement.

In the spring of 1969, another opportunity was presented to Jackie and me. Rex Tice, the regional supervisor of law enforcement for the Service's northeast region, called me to ask if I might be interested in moving east. Rex was originally from Wisconsin, and after working and living in many parts of the country, was now headquartered in Boston.

"Are you interested in the agent-in-charge position in New Hampshire?"

"Give me a day or two to decide."

Jackie and I got out our atlas. As always, she soon had books and pamphlets that explained all about New Hampshire: its history, stone walls, mountains, and coastline. As much as we liked our home and friends and life in western Minnesota, New Hampshire sounded terribly interesting, too interesting to turn down. By June of 1969, we had again picked up and moved, this time to Concord, New Hampshire.

Our first days in New England were spent making quick little trips to see the ocean and the Old Man of the Mountain near Mount Washington, and enjoying the New England history that we were eager and ready to soak up.

But before I knew it, I was back on the road all over the East coast checking sea duck hunters, helping the state put on conservation officer training sessions and becoming involved in the investigation and prosecution of interstate deer violators. I found that the 100-mile trip I might have taken into North or South Dakota now carried me over two or three state borders, each state having its own regulations and ways of doing business.

Tide's out

I had lots to learn in my new assignment. I had worked on Lakes Michigan, Superior, and Erie, and had been up and down the Mississippi and all over the Missouri. But this big "lake"—the Atlantic— was, to say the least, quite impressive.

I was warned about five- to ten-foot tides, shoals, fog, salt, and weather. I learned how to launch and operate good-sized boats offshore and in the tidal waters, like the Great Bay of New Hampshire. I learned all about mud flats, and how fast you can lose your water when the tide decides to take all the water out from under you. I had some good New Hampshire warden teachers who had ridden the tides for many years. One told me, "The water can run off like a scalded cat, and you better be somewhere else."

Now I headed up to Merrymeeting Bay near Brunswick, Maine, for an early teal season. I watched a hunter in a boat shoot an illegal mallard, pull the feathers off the bird, and shove the identifying hide down into the mud just below the surface of the shallow tidal waters. I was watching the hunter with a 30-power scope from the shore. Then I saw the same hunter stalk an injured Canada goose, put it in a gunnysack, and hide the goose under some decoys in his boat.

I decided I'd better launch my boat and get to the hunter before I ran out of water. By the time I got to him, the tide was going fast. I seized the goose and some breasted-out ducks that couldn't be identified. Then I turned toward the spot in the water where the nervous hunter had buried the hide and the feathers.

"I see your luck is running out just like the water," I said.

The mallard feathers and hide now lay completely exposed on the mud, exposed to the world and the special agents of the U.S. Fish and Wildlife Service.

It wasn't this hunter's day in the sun. I guess I had already learned that people are people, in New England too.

The chase

Things had changed for me by the seventies and eighties. I made the move into a supervisor role, and into the Boston office in the early seventies, then to Minneapolis as assistant special agent-in-charge of the midwest region in '74, and back to Boston as the agent-in-charge in 1978. All this took me somewhat, but not entirely, out of the field as an enforcement officer. I wasn't actively involved in the *chase*, but I was in the background watching every move.

Have you ever followed a friend by car, headed for some location that was unfamiliar to you? Suddenly, the car you are following is gone. Your friend made the light, you didn't. He turned left, you were blocked by traffic. And even though your friend did everything possible to help you keep him in sight, it didn't work. His car disappeared or her car vanished in the traffic ahead, not to be seen for hours or maybe until the next day. (In one of my house moves, my truck and several drivers helping me to move became separated and didn't get back together again until the next day. It can happen.)

Picture this: You are given the task of following a car for 900 miles. You must follow it down interstate highways, back alleys, through restaurant and motel parking lots, through big city thoroughfares, back streets, and toll booths. This chase must be unobserved by the chasee.

Surveillance must be done in broad daylight and also at night. You must never lose sight of your quarry. If you can imagine such a chase, then you will partially understand the difficulty experienced by Maine wardens and special agents of the U.S. Fish and Wildlife Service when they perform such a feat.

Buying or selling protected migratory birds is a felony under the Migratory Bird Treaty Act. For almost a year, Maine wardens were aware of a middle-aged, heavyset man, an antique dealer named Costello. He was circulating the state buying mounted migratory birds for resale.

The Maine wardens contacted federal agents when they suspected that Costello was planning to resell the birds to someone in Pennsylvania. Soon both state and federal officers were monitoring his transactions and contacts in Maine and in Pennsylvania. They were looking for information on Costello's market in Pennsylvania.

By the end of the summer, Costello had accumulated enough

mounted birds and illegal animals to fill the back seat of his $22,000 white Lincoln Continental Mark VI. Inside information indicated that Costello would be headed south any day. He made several apparently false starts, but always returned to his antique shop residence.

In the meantime, the only lead from Pennsylvania was some sketchy information about a Maine antique dealer who had tried to sell an owl to a furniture company somewhere in Pittsburgh several years ago. Nothing concrete was uncovered.

Suddenly, early one morning, Costello was on his way south. He had removed the back seat of his car and filled the rear end with mounted birds and animals. He had paid over $1,000 for the illegal load of wildlife.

Two Maine warden cars and one agent cruiser started the surveillance. No one car followed Costello long enough for him to become suspicious that he was being tailed. Other agent cars filled in and with constant radio contact, the officers continued the long chase without real problems all the way to the New Jersey–Pennsylvania border. Other federal agents waited near Harrisburg to assist in the surveillance.

But at one point, Costello made several unusual turns after stopping at a restaurant. He disappeared. Thinking quickly, the agents made contact with the state police helicopter squad. Just when hope of seeing the big white car was about gone, the helicopter spotted Costello back on the interstate. He was just entering a toll booth headed toward Pittsburgh.

"There he is!" One of the relieved agents sighted him again on the busy highway. Surveillance continued.

Soon the big white Lincoln was cruising into downtown Pittsburgh. Using four different state and federal cars, the officers were still on his tail. The Maine officers had come all the way. All officers seemed to sense they were close to their destination. Costello turned onto a side street. Suddenly, as before, he vanished. Like a vapor cloud, he was gone.

The four officer cars met back where they had last seen the Continental. They felt pretty bad about losing their quarry after all their efforts up to this point. The Maine officers started back home, feeling pretty low.

"You know, there's a furniture warehouse about two blocks up that street," said one of the remaining agents, over a tasteless cup of coffee. "I went right by it several minutes ago. Wasn't there information about this guy possibly selling the birds to a furniture company?"

Everyone went back into action. A hasty trip to the warehouse indicated that people were leaving for the day. It was quitting time, 4:30 P.M.

One of the agents went quickly to a telephone and called the warehouse. The phone rang and rang. It appeared there would be no answer. Just when the agent was about to hang up, a woman said, "Hello." She must have been walking out and decided to answer one more call.

"Hi there, my name is Ron Bilford and I was supposed to meet a Mr. Costello at your warehouse at 3:00 P.M. I'm out here not far from your warehouse, but got delayed. I had some car trouble. Could you tell me if Mr. Costello is there or if he was there this afternoon?" (The agent didn't tell the woman his car trouble was *lost* car trouble.)

"Oh yes, Mr. Costello was here about 3:30, finished his business and left here just a few minutes ago."

"Thank you, ma'am. Thank you so much."

The next morning, agents arrived at the furniture warehouse. After a few minutes of discussion with the manager, he brought out the mounted birds and animals voluntarily. A check stub indicated that Costello had been paid over $5,000 for the illegal wildlife.

Costello pleaded guilty in federal court. He paid a small fine and was put on probation for one year, but his $22,000 car was forfeited to the government. The furniture company stopped payment on the $5,000 check. They also paid a $500 fine.

There are wildlife outlaws everywhere

After 1974, federal agents were no longer called U.S. game management agents. Instead we were given a new title: Special Agents of the U.S. Fish and Wildlife Service. We were divided into thirteen law-enforcement districts in the United States. The man in charge of each district was called the SAC, or Special Agent-in-Charge. His assistant was called the ASAC. In 1974, I returned to Minneapolis as the ASAC for the seventh district which was comprised of Minnesota, Wisconsin, Illinois, Indiana, Ohio, and Michigan.

During my four years back in Minnesota, our district agents came down pretty hard on some of the wildlife commercializers. Our most potent weapon against these outdoor outlaws was undercover work.

During this period we investigated and prosecuted a father and son who killed hawks and owls and sold them through the mails. (Selling

protected migratory birds is a felony.) In a jury trial before the chief
district judge, the defendants were found guilty, sentenced to pay large
fines, and were put on probation for several years. The father said on
the stand, "I was only protecting my property." Taxidermists all over
the state, who were operating illegally, were also raided at this time.
The taxidermist business in Minnesota has been "cleaner," and taxidermists have generally complied with the law ever since.

Let me mention some of the other cases that proved interesting
in those days. An Indiana mayor was prosecuted for ordering the killing
of hundreds of purple martens that were roosting in a tree overhanging
the city hall. Wisconsin commercial fishermen were prosecuted for
illegally taking and selling protected lake trout in their nets. There was
also the break-up of a Michigan-Ohio "wild animal for sale" ring. This
case took several years to investigate and prosecute. It involved the

Special Agent Dave Duncan prepares to take carcasses of timber wolves, illegally killed in area of Duluth, Minnesota, to locker in Minneapolis area to be held as evidence. Man who wrote notes describing his hatred toward wolves was eventually convicted, partly through matching samples of his handwriting. Special agents deal with numerous cases involving endangered species.

illegal sale of rabbits, birds, deer, and even coon carcasses for the table. A former governor of Illinois was apprehended shooting mourning doves over a baited field.

There even was an investigation of several eagles bludgeoned to death in an Ohio zoo. The culprits broke into the zoo and through the bars of the eagles' cage to do their thoughtless act. And I remember the case of an often-prosecuted Minnesota man who was sentenced to one year in a federal penitentiary for killing an eagle and attempting to sell it to undercover agents for the highly valuable feathers.

In each of these cases, both state officers and federal agents worked closely to bring the guilty parties before the appropriate court. Seldom does the federal agent work on a major wildlife case without state assistance and cooperation.

During my transitions—from state officer to agent to agent-in-charge of a state to ASAC and SAC, and from midwest to east and back and forth—I found the secret to any wildlife enforcement success was caring about the resources and attempting to understand what makes them tick.

I also found that the average midwesterner thought the East coast was paved entirely in blacktop and that wilderness places did not exist in New York or Boston. The average New Englander had never gotten farther west than Buffalo, and he thought that if you were from Wisconsin or Minnesota, Wyoming was just over the hill. A Concord, New Hampshire butcher, hearing we came from Wisconsin said, "I've been to Wisconsin. Awfully flat out there." I asked him what part of Wisconsin he had visited. He said, "Cleveland."

I think that moving about the country opened my eyes to many new concepts and to all kinds of outdoor wonders. Since my beginning as a state officer, I had felt a certain closeness to the wild country and the wild animals I had been empowered to protect. I have found that other wildlife officers and wildlife professionals share this same feeling. Children especially care about wild things and they want to become involved with the outdoors. I have tried to work with children, helping them become involved, all through my career.

In my wildlife enforcement travels, I have rubbed shoulders with many special people who care a great deal about the kinds of wild places and animals I care about. My associations with so many of these caring people—teachers, veterinarians, scientists, police and other law-enforcement officers, businessmen, laborers—have caused me to have faith in people when the going has been tough and the job of protecting the outdoors particularly overwhelming and unpopular. This book would be incomplete without a few stories about some of these special people.

A second chance for eagles

Carl Madson boarded the 727 in Minneapolis headed for Boston. He was carrying an incubator. At Boston, he transferred to another plane and was off to Bangor, Maine. The incubator received first-class treatment by everyone, even though Carl and his special cargo traveled, by government regulations, in the coach.

The contents of the incubator were unusual—three fertile bald eagle eggs. Carl, a veteran biologist for the U.S. F&W Service, carried with him permits from our office and the states involved. The permits authorized him to possess and transfer three eagle eggs from Wisconsin to Maine. The eggs had been taken carefully from three different nests in three different parts of Wisconsin. They were removed from nests where more than one egg was being hatched by the parent eagles.

Reproduction in the Wisconsin nests had been good. Madson had brought the fertile eggs to Maine as a closely watched experiment. The plan was to plant fertile eggs in active eagle nests in Maine. The end result, it was hoped, would be young eaglets hatching to improve the disappearing eagle population in the Northeast.

When Carl got to Maine, another F&W Service biologist, Frank Gramlich, met Carl and took him by truck to the remote Washington County areas he knew so well. There, a trained climber gingerly carried the fertile eggs up into three carefully selected, secluded eagle nests.

By 1972, there was virtually no bald eagle reproduction in the state of Maine. The seclusion that is necessary for bald eagles to build their 500- to 4,000-pound nests and to hatch out one, two, or three eaglets, was still present in the wilderness areas of northeastern Maine. Maine had the only active eagle nests left in the New England states. Now Maine's reproduction had all but disappeared.

The problem was DDT. Adult birds, four years old or older, continued to mate and lay eggs in the fifty-plus, fairly widespread nests in Washington County. But the eggs were not hatching. The adult birds had consumed in their mostly dead or dying fish diet large quantities of DDT. The DDT caused the eggs to break under the eight- to twelve-pound weight of one of the birds. It appeared to be the end for all bald eagles on the northeast coast.

But very restrictive federal measures were soon taken, banning the massive use of DDT in the areas along the migration routes of these birds with the seven- and eight-foot wingspans. Reproduction was still years away.

The U.S. Fish and Wildlife Service decided to try something quite unusual. Eagle reproduction in Wisconsin and Minnesota was among the best in the nation. DDT had been restricted in its use in the Midwest for some time. Eagle eggs there were not breaking under the weight of the birds as they were in the Northeast. Soon we would see if the adoptive parents would accept the eggs, hatch them, and raise these "foreign" eaglets.

The eggs were accepted. The Madsons and the Gramlichs and many others working with the birds had done their job well. They were professionals who cared. But my involvement in the story is the sad part.

Two of the three eaglets grew to fly for a short time in the wilds of Maine. I became involved when my office was called. The special agent in Maine said sadly, "Both the young eagles have been found shot to death on the Penobscot River." The young transplant birds had been banded after hatching. The bands identified the two gunned-down birds as our Wisconsin imports.

The young eagles had survived being removed from one nest, taken 2,000 miles by air, being placed with loving care into new nests, accepted and raised by Downeast eagle parents. They made their first flights and a start toward becoming the nucleus of a new northeast bald eagle population—all to end because of some unthinking, uncaring shooter. I don't use the word hunter. A shooter probably received some small thrill from shooting two large, hawk-like birds.

His ignorance was a tragedy and our nation's loss. But it won't diminish the determination of those who care to do something for the creatures of the wilderness. Due to the control of DDT and the continued, determined efforts of people like Madson and Gramlich, natural eagle reproduction was again putting young eagles into the skies over Maine and the East coast by the late 1970s. There are now over fifty producing nests in northeastern Maine, according to the 1984 annual eagle survey conducted by the F&W Service and the state of Maine.

The strength of an eaglet

"OK, send up the bird." Pat was calling down from eighty feet above. We were now at the critical point. I had placed the powerful young eagle into a burlap sack with its head sticking out. I had taped the bird's wings to its body to reduce the chances of any injury in its endless struggle for freedom. I wore heavy leather gloves and avoided the eaglet's strong and quick beak.

Pat Redig, veterinarian, falconer, bird surgeon, pilot, and now a climber of eighty-foot pines, waited above, only a few feet from the huge bald eagle nest. Pat had lowered a rope to me. I reached out and snapped on the eagle held securely in the bag. Pat started to raise the eagle toward him. Above, mama and papa eagle soared, calling Pat and me many names—names we didn't understand, but knew weren't complimentary.

In the nest already was a lone brood. That young bird sat nervously, watching Pat with its big brown eyes. We just hoped the addition of this new mouth to feed would be accepted by all who called this 700-pound nest home.

Pat started to raise the bag and eagle toward him. The parents continued to soar, scream, and occasionally dive. The one baby in the nest, still not quite able to fly, became visibly more nervous as Pat raised its new brother toward the nest. The bird in the nest hopped out onto some large branches that the nest was resting on. This made *me* somewhat nervous. We didn't want to harm it. Our plan and all our past efforts were to increase the eagle population, not jeopardize it. So far everything had gone pretty well.

The eagle in the bag had come from a nest farther south in the state of Wisconsin. A howling windstorm had blown over an eagle nest tree on one of the national wildlife refuges. Refuge and Wildlife Service employees there soon surveyed the damage and found the eagle tree down. They knew from having observed the nest from a distance during the preceding four or five weeks that the nest was active. Two young had hatched and were soon ready for flight.

The Refuge people found the two young birds under the tree. One was injured; the second appeared unhurt. The injured bird was sent quickly to the University of Minnesota where Dr. Gary Duke runs one of the finest and most up-to-date bird rehabilitation centers in the country. His staff diagnosed the young bird's injury as only a broken leg. Everything else appeared to be okay.

The second, uninjured eagle was left on the ground for several days. Many young eagles somehow get out of the nest before they are ready to fly. Many of them are still cared for by their parents, and some do survive to fly.

But after several days of observation, it appeared the parents were not coming back. Their nest was gone, and to them, so were their young. The second eaglet was also sent to the lab at the University of Minnesota. Both birds were cared for there while we looked for their new home.

I felt it would be only right to return these two eagles to the nests where, several years before, we had taken eggs for the state of Maine.

Maine's eagle reproduction by this time had started anew. DDT was now strictly forbidden as an aerial spray in the forest areas of the Northeast.

After several weeks of looking, we found the right nests. First, the nests had to be active, and had to have only one fledgling eagle. This meant the parents were actively feeding their one youngster. We were concerned about injecting our new young bird into a two-eaglet family; it might present a problem. Although three birds sometimes are hatched, it appears that three seldom survive for whatever reason (maybe lack of feed). Two usually do.

We found our tree near Cable, Wisconsin. While we waited for the injured leg of the first youngster to heal, we made our arrangements with the local warden, George Phillips, and flew the first youngster to Wisconsin.

Now you and I are back at the nest tree. Pat has pulled the young bird up to where he can reach it and remove it from the bag. Pat is so experienced with handling birds that it seems to be no trick pulling an eagle from a bag. Nothing to it, eighty feet in the air, adults crying and swooping, another young hopping around nervously. Pat, wearing climbing spikes, hangs next to the tree by his leather climbing belt. And he is taking pictures!

I hear George say, "Pat has the eaglet out of the bag and has untaped the wings." I knew how firmly Pat had to hold the bird. An hour before, when I prepared to carry him from the car the mile back to the tree, I could barely hold the bird as it struggled to regain its freedom. The eaglet was now ten weeks old. It was almost the size of an adult. (It would be four or more years before it would show the white head of the mature bald eagle.)

Pat has now put the bird in the nest. The natural born eaglet still sits out on the branch nervously. Pat starts down. We clear out of the area and let the adult birds return to the nest.

"I'd love to be here to see the reaction of the adult birds when they come back to see if their baby is all right, and find he's become twins," I tell George and Pat.

It worked. Within a month, the adopted eagle was flying. It was reported to George that he was seen flying with the adults high over the trees. We knew it was our bird because he carried a colored ribbon-like wing marker that showed when he was in the air.

Eagle number two was another story. We found another nest from which we had taken an egg several years before. My good friends Bob and Myke Mercier, who run a boys' camp several miles from the nest, were very interested in the transplant. Each year they took boys from the camp to the lake where the eagle nest was located to see, from a distance, the nest and the eagle activity.

Pat and I brought in the second eaglet. Its leg was now fully healed. Pat was concerned that this bird was now very large and almost ready to fly. We flew in with the eaglet to a small field near the camp and the nest site—this time near Minong, Wisconsin. We stopped at the camp to let the boys catch a quick look at the only live eaglet they would probably ever see. Remarks like, "Holy cow, a real eagle!" and "Look at the size of his eyes!" spiced up the morning flag-raising ceremony.

We went to the nest site with our eagle and carried it to the eagle tree. We knew from a previous flight that we had one young already in the nest. Pat climbed the tree as the adult birds circled high above. We were in for a surprise.

Just as Pat reached the nest, the young eagle in the nest fluttered out, half flying, half sailing. The young bird landed safely at my feet next to the lake. "I've got it!" I shouted, as I carefully captured the eagle with a landing net. We replaced it in the nest, where it stayed. Then Pat placed our recuperated bird in the nest.

Another surprise. Just as the new addition was released into the nest, it flew out of the tree and out across the nearby marsh. It landed shakily in a tree just across the marsh. We knew we couldn't leave the young bird there. It did not know how to feed itself. The adults would assuredly not claim this new bird as their own. Bob, Pat, and I converged on the eagle that had just made its first solo flight. The bird flew again, across to the other side of the marsh. We waded the marsh and caught the bird as it tumbled from a tree into the water.

This time we placed the new flier in a smaller tree just below the nest tree. We had to pray that the adults would find this helpless bird as they often do when their own young take premature flights. Our efforts were worth the gamble. Bob and Myke called me one day about a month later.

"We saw the eagle flying. It was marked with the white wing ribbon. It was flying with two adult eagles. It was beautiful."

Some may wonder why we took the time and spent the money to replant these helpless young birds back into the wild. We did it because we did not want to condemn these otherwise healthy, future national-emblem birds to a life in a zoo, domesticated and caged.

Some eagles—because they are flightless, crippled, partially blind, or because they have been held in captivity too long—must become zoo birds. Those you see in zoos are birds held under permit from the U.S. Fish and Wildlife Service. But eagles and other birds that can make it in the wild should be given a chance to do so.

If you have ever watched a soaring eagle dive after a rabbit at ninety miles per hour, if you have experienced the thrill of standing close to an eagle or have held an eaglet prior to its release and felt its yearning to be free, then you know why people care about eagles. I believe they should.

Strictly for the birds

In every state in the nation, there are people who take care of injured birds. They must possess permits from both the state and federal government to take in the injured birds and rehabilitate them back into the wild. These people must have certain facilities and certain skills before they can effectively take care of injured birds. Dr. Gary Duke and his staff at the veterinary school of the University of Minnesota are some of the most skilled bird rehabilitators in the nation. They have developed very modern holding and treatment facilities. Their specific expertise is the care and rehabilitation of raptors, particularly eagles; but they do handle many other types of birds each year, putting them back into the outdoors to make it on their own.

I worked with these professionals while I was the assistant special agent-in-charge in Minneapolis in the late 1970s. During that time, I saw the university take in hundreds of injured (mostly shot) eagles from all over the nation. Many of these birds were later returned to the wild for a second chance.

In their highly technical facilities, Dr. Duke and his staff care for one-winged eagles, one-eyed eagles, and even eagles with only one leg. Birds that cannot be rehabilitated back into the wild usually end up in a zoo or wildlife exhibit where people can finally see them up close. Duke also supervises work with peregrine falcons, hawks, owls, and other birds, but eagles seem to be his specialty.

I have been on hand several times when we released rehabilitated eagles from one of the Minnesota cliffs overlooking the Mississippi River. I was there when Gary tossed powerful eagles into the air. We watched the graceful birds catch an updraft and sail off majestically over the trees for another chance to survive.

There are veterinarians, Audubon staffs, zoo and science center employees all over the nation who, under federal and state permits,

Bald eagle, after rehabilitation in lab at University of Minnesota, St. Paul, is released by Dr. Gary Duke south of city on bluffs overlooking Mississippi River while press and television cameras record the action. Hundreds of birds have been returned to wild after treatment at University, under cooperative agreement with U.S. Fish and Wildlife Service. *Photo by U.S. Fish and Wildlife Service*

put birds back into the wild with their thoughtful efforts. There are also many private-citizen permittees who become qualified and build facilities to care for and rehabilitate wildlife. I'd like to tell you about a special guy in Springfield, Massachusetts, who is *strictly* for the birds.

Dick Lucius is a retired fireman. He has dedicated his life not only to caring for birds, but to teaching people—mostly children—about birds. He talks about raptors—hawks, owls, peregrine falcons, and particularly eagles. This talented man explains the nobility of raptors: "Raptors have unique abilities and can add spice to your lives."

Dick demonstrates the special qualities of these birds by showing his audiences the real thing. He has a permit to possess and transport a peregrine falcon, golden eagle, red-tailed hawk, great-horned owl, and prairie falcon. Children from all over western Massachusetts and some of the surrounding states see these birds up close for the first time.

Dick doesn't teach that it would be nice to have one of these birds as a pet. Instead, he speaks about the marvelous qualities of raptors. He tells how they hunt and how they survive in the wilderness. Dick captivates his audiences with his birds and with his knowledge of them.

I once watched this man hold a group of wildlife officers spellbound. We all had some prior experience handling raptors, but were thrilled when Dick brought out Keneu, the golden eagle he respects and understands. Golden eagles are not easy to handle; this golden eagle trusted this special human being. She put her head alongside Dick's head. She performed no people tricks.

None of Dick's birds are taught to perform tricks. Instead, he exhibits them to show their wildness and magnificence. Dick shows these birds as birds of character, not as pets, not as animals who must perform tricks to show their value to the world, or their right to exist.

"Only persons with special permits can possess these birds," Dick explains, "and permits are not issued for someone to make a pet of these majestic birds." He also teaches that "these birds are not flawless. They, like human beings, make mistakes and sometimes cause problems for people." But when Dick Lucius, a man who cares, completes his hour of spellbinding instruction, everyone knows that he *is* strictly for the birds.

It takes one to catch one

After four good years in Minneapolis–St. Paul, it looked like we were going to move one more time. The SAC position in Boston was becoming vacant. Even though we enjoyed Minnesota and the Midwest, our home country, we had also fallen in love with New England. I applied for the job, knowing our son Eric was now in his first year of college and our daughter Stacy was graduating from high school in the spring. This time we moved in the fall. Jackie's only comment was, "I've missed the ocean and the mountains." It was 1978.

I inherited a small district, with six small states, a small number of agents (only ten), and a small budget to operate on. The agents worked hard and the state officers in all the New England states were eager to work with us in going after the wildlife commercializer. It wasn't long before we started to have some success apprehending and prosecuting interstate deer rings, illegal importers of endangered species, illegal fur dealers, and illegal fishermen who did their dirty work back and forth across the Canadian border. Let me tell you about the illegal trout fishermen.

Crossing the Canadian–United States border in an aircraft without the proper clearances and failing to report all wildlife imported are

Promotions bring new assignments. In his role as Special Agent in Charge (SAC), Swendsen had to spend far more time than he would have liked away from the field and behind his desk. *Photo by Bill Whalen, U.S. Fish and Wildlife Service*

violations of U.S. and Canadian regulations. All hunters and fishermen who fly into Canada and return to the United States must file a flight plan, clear with U.S. customs officials, and declare on a special form all fish and game brought back into this country.

There are, of course, those "sportsmen" who bring back overbags and illegally taken wildlife. They do not follow the aircraft or the declaration rules, and they feel pretty safe flying back and forth across the international border. The penalties for not landing where planned or not clearing with customs can be severe. They can result in the forfeiture of the aircraft.

The Maine wardens and our agents became aware of some U.S. citizens who were flying into Canada in their light aircraft (float planes), catching large overbags of trout, and returning to the United States. On their return, the float planes would first land at some small uninhabited lake in Maine and unload their overbags of trout. They would then fly to their designated flight plan site and report in to customs. When they reported their catch, they had only their legal limits of fish.

The float plane operators loaded up new fishermen the next weekend and repeated the game over and over. With the maze of tiny Maine lakes along the border, apprehending these sophisticated wildlife outlaws had to be difficult—so difficult that they felt pretty safe in their operation, which had gone on for some time.

The Maine officers, customs agents, and our special agents teamed up to put the squeeze on these fly-in, sneak-out fishermen. I told you I inherited a small operation, but I didn't mention one piece of equipment we had in the district that compensated for our smallness: a beautiful Cessna 185 float plane (and one of our agents was the pilot).

Just before a big holiday weekend, our plane and several agents headed for the border. Agents and Maine wardens monitored the suspected float planes when they left their base stations with fishermen aboard. On the radio they reported, "They are heading for Canadian waters." When the suspected float planes and their fishermen returned to the United States, our plane was in the air, following them to their preplanned first-stop lake.

"They're landing on Little Bass Lake," our pilot reported on his radio. When the suspected aircraft landed on this small wilderness lake that was not listed on their flight plan, and not legal for them to land on without clearance through customs, the federal aircraft landed right behind them. Our agent-pilot, accompanied by a Maine warden, boarded the returning aircraft almost before their propellers stopped turning. The pilots were turned over to the customs officials and charged with failure to land at the proper place for customs clearance. They were

Special Agents Tom Wharton (left) and Clyde Bolin of the U.S. Fish and Wildlife Service prepare to take off from small airport in Newburyport, Massachusetts for an air patrol and survey over the Parker River Wildlife Refuge. The walkie-talkie Wharton holds can be used on special frequencies to talk with agents on ground. *Photo by U.S. Fish and Wildlife Service*

fined and went on the record; a second offense would result in loss of their expensive aircraft.

I'm sure these pilots were surprised to see another plane land beside them on their remote little lake. I expect their surprise turned to something else when they saw a state and federal officer approach their aircraft before the waves hit the shore. It certainly was true that it took a plane to catch a plane.

Near the end of a long trail

Jackie and I landed back in New England for the last leg of our fish and wildlife enforcement career. The last years were to prove undercover work was the real key to catching those who had the most to gain from exploiting the wildlife. In a short time, our New England agents and Massachusetts and New Hampshire state officers broke up a money-making deer poaching ring in Massachusetts—a country-store venison and small-game selling operation that had gone on for many years. Our agents also extracted a civil penalty of over $100,000 from an illegal shoe importer for illegally importing snakeskin shoes that were protected by the Endangered Species Act.

In a secure storage room, Dave Swendsen (right) and Ron Varney inventory a shipment of shoes that was illegally imported to Boston area. Shoes were made from skins of reticulated pythons, an endangered species. Importer forfeited $100,000 worth of shoes and paid fine of $15,000. *Photo by Bill Whalen, U.S. Fish and Wildlife Service*

With a new administration in 1981, the Department of the Interior was reorganized. The new assistant secretary dissolved the thirteen well-functioning SAC offices and reverted to the old seven-region system. It was in the name of economy and efficiency. The newly placed special agents-in-charge of the nation had to meet a former prerequisite that now was put into full force. Each must have at least two years of Washington, D.C. experience. Because of other multiregional experience or state experience, waivers had previously been granted for some of the SACs who, like myself, had not had a Washington education. Now those waivers were cancelled as a new leadership came into power in the division under James Watt and his assistant, Ray Arnett.

I was fortunate. With less than two years remaining, I received a new title. I soon became the Special Project Officer. I was asked to help write my own job description. My last years were spent training other department officers, setting up special task force raids, and coordinating conferences and meetings.

I also spent the last several waterfowl seasons checking hunters in the field and becoming more personally active in the field-enforcement investigations. No more staff meetings and budget fights and ceiling cuts. No more program management meetings and last-minute spending sessions. It was good to once again have a chance to pull on the waders and routinely become involved in field apprehensions and takedowns. It was hard to believe I had been a rookie game warden in Wisconsin almost thirty years ago. Time had sure flown by.

"I guess I've passed through the rookie stage now," I told Jackie.

I found I still had things to learn, as I moved out onto a Massachusetts bog one night to check late duck hunters. I felt I had to get closer to the two hunters I had just watched shoot ten minutes past shooting hours. I figured if they shot again, they would be in trouble.

I carefully picked my way through the water areas in the bog, but not carefully enough. Just as four geese flew over my head and sailed out over the two hunters, I stepped into a bottomless hole. Water went up to my armpits. My raincoat over my waders prevented the muddy water from pouring rapidly into the waders. But I was loaded down

A three-year undercover operation led to the arrest of importer who had illegally brought raw ivory into the Lower 48 from Alaska. Some of this evidence was stored in a bank security box and was recovered by agents under a federal search warrant. This ivory was part of a shipment of 10,000 pounds to several states. *Photo by Bill Whalen, U.S. Fish and Wildlife Service*

with a .357 in a shoulder holster and a 12-gauge shotgun (for effect). I reached out with the shotgun to a nearby bog clump and pulled myself up out of the hole.

Just as I got out of the muck, the two hunters emptied their guns at the geese. It was twenty minutes after shooting hours. Several hunters on the shore, who had let the geese fly by without shooting, called out, "Hey, it's after hours."

I approached the two hunters and greeted them as they headed for shore. They had little to say when I identified myself and advised them that underneath all the mud and grime was a U.S. special agent who would write them up for shooting after hours. They explained their embarrassment later.

"We're both police officers here with the local department. I'm the sergeant. My hunting partner is the police inspector."

After working to coordinate a task force operation with New York State officers, I ended up checking hunters one night along a tidal river near Kings Park, Long Island. (Tides there surprise a newcomer as they rise as high as eight feet when the wind is blowing strongly from the northeast.) Homeowners along the river had been complaining about hunters shooting after dark and close to their houses.

I was on one side of the river and the young state officer was on the other side watching for late hunters. I located two hunters who didn't seem ready to go home when hunting hours came to a close and the moon started to come out. They shot a mallard fifty minutes after shooting time was over. I watched it spiral into the ground in the moonlight.

My only problem was that I was fifty yards away, across the now muddy river. I had only one recourse. Thinking back to little Ed's words way back when, I remembered, "always on the offense."

I shined my not too bright flashlight across the river at them and shouted, "I'm a federal agent. There are officers also on your side of the river. Get in your boat and come to this landing. And bring that mallard you just shot with you."

Knowing it would be easy for them to get into their boat and disappear into the marsh grass, I was somewhat surprised when one man answered, "Yes sir," and over they came to get their summons. Little Ed had also said, "Don't lie to them." I hadn't. There were officers on the other side of the river, even if *he* was four miles downriver and my radio had quit functioning.

What you see is not always what you get

To end this chapter in my life, I want to tell you about one more episode that I was not involved in; fellow agents down south put it together. This story shows the importance of undercover work to all enforcement operations. Undercover work makes it possible to move in on the real wildlife outlaw in his well protected, native area. Without undercover work, most of the real wildlife outlaws would never come to court.

Illegal wildlife sales gross millions of dollars each year for people who have developed this lucrative and reasonably safe way to exploit the wilderness. In recent years, some of the bad guys have been caught. Courts are still pretty slow to come down hard on those convicted, but some large fines and a few jail sentences are beginning to be imposed. First, the illegal commercializer has to be apprehended. As in the apprehension of drug runners and drug dealers, undercover operations are often the only way the culprits are caught.

Alligators can be worth a lot of money. Although they've made a partial comeback in some of the southeastern states in recent years, they are still on the endangered species list. Not long ago, some of our fellow agents in the southeast part of the nation moved in on and arrested some big-time illegal dealers in alligators. These dealers were operating across state lines between Alabama, through Mississippi and into Louisiana.

The alligator bandits had been killing as many as ten alligators a night, using lights and high-powered rifles in the Alabama swamps. They were looking for a better market to unload their illegally obtained hides for a quick profit. They had been selling illegal hides for some time, but now were looking for a good, safe contact who would buy their whole truckload for a good price.

After several months, they found just the contact they were looking for, because he was making himself easy to be found. He was Ruby Rabono, and he would pay a good price for just about anything the alligator bandits could deliver. Ruby was in fact a special agent for the U. S. Fish and Wildlife Service. He had been setting himself up with a false front as an illegal dealer in wildlife and wildlife products for more then six months. Ruby posed as a businessman in another city across the state line in Louisiana.

Soon the greedy alligator bandits and Ruby got to know each other. They made a few small deals, feeling each other's operation out. When

Ruby felt the bandits were ready, he told them he would buy their whole truckload of alligator hides for a good price. But he wanted them to know that he didn't want to get caught by the feds going across state lines.

"I hope you know it's a violation of the federal Lacey Act, taking those hides across state lines. We've got to be damn careful."

"We know all about the Lacey Act," the bandits replied. "We can deal with the feds, they won't catch us. How about some hot outboard motors and a little pot thrown in on the deal, just to make it interesting?" Ruby told them he would buy anything if the price was right.

Special arrangements were made for the bandits to deliver the alligator hides to Ruby's warehouse in his town, across the state line. The bandits told Ruby many times they didn't care where they had to deliver the hides and other "goodies." "Just have the cash ready," they said.

So, on the day arranged, the bandits rolled up to Ruby's warehouse with their truck loaded to the top with alligator hides and a few sample outboard motors. The motors were taken from some sleeping citizens' boats one night.

Ruby's big shiny Cadillac was parked at the warehouse door; he and his "hide graders" waited inside for the bandits to arrive. (The warehouse had been rented for the day. The Cadillac belonged to Ruby's car-dealer friend.)

When the truck pulled up, the big doors opened and the bandits backed their loot right into the warehouse. All hands went to hauling out the hides and spreading them on the warehouse floor. Ruby's men then went to grading the hides. The "graders" in reality were other agents, state wildlife officers and several deputy sheriffs, there to help make the arrest.

Ruby and the head bandit got together to make the deal. It was to be so much per hide, all in cash. Ruby had spent several hours convincing his chiefs that he would need a large roll of "flash" money, plus enough actual cash to pay off the bandits. The bandits would hold the actual cash only long enough to count it.

Once the deal was made and the cash had actually changed hands, the local police and sheriff would, on signal, burst into the warehouse and make the arrest. The signal was for one of Ruby's agents to go to the door and take off his cap. At that point another agent, stationed in a nearby window, would call on his portable radio and bring in the police and sheriff.

Ruby and the head bandit were looking at the hides and getting ready to make the deal.

"Noticed we went right by the police station on our way into your warehouse, Ruby. In our town we don't have to worry about the police. We have a little arrangement going with them. We got them in our pocket. What kinda cooperation ya got here?"

"First I better let you count your money. Then I'll tell you what real cooperation is."

The deal specified a certain amount of money for twenty more outboard motors to be picked up later at an Alabama address. Ruby was waiting for the address before the takedown. When Ruby passed the roll of bills, his agent now knew he had all the information. He gave the signal. Nothing happened. Ruby had to stall for a little time. This crew of armed alligator bandits could be mean without backup support from the police and sheriff.

Ruby had to think fast, but that was just part of his everyday duty.

"You think you have the police in your pocket. We're better off than that. The local police come here to the warehouse almost every day. In fact, if they come in while we're moving motors and hides, don't worry. They're in on the deal. They know all about our operation." (He certainly was telling the truth.)

Just a few moments later, the police and sheriff did arrive.

"Just keep working boys," the head bandit said to his men. "The police here are just like they are back home."

Once all the illegal hides and motors were offloaded onto the warehouse floor, the police and Ruby's men made their move. Before the bandits knew what was going on, the "friendly" police had them arrested, cuffed, and searched for weapons. Ruby personally searched the head bandit and recovered the roll of government funds.

A quick call was made to "not in the pocket" agents and state police in Alabama, and a raid took place to recover the stolen outboard motors. Stolen property was still being retrieved days later. Ruby would no longer see the bandits, except as a government witness at their trial. Now it was up to the court.

PART IV

THE WILDLIFE OUTLAW

How he gets away

Now that I've hauled you over the dusty back roads of our nation's wilderness and across its waters from Wisconsin's crystal-clear Shell Lake to the crashing rollers of the Atlantic, I feel it is important to devote a part of this book exclusively to my experiences with the wildlife outlaw.

As I look back on my career, I must admit I feel a certain anger toward those who, without regard for others and without regard for the nation's future, take from the outdoors with no thought to the damage they are doing.

Their goal, almost without exception, is money. Wildlife can bring big profits—profits far beyond what most of us can imagine. Most Americans hear little about wolf pelts that sell for $1,000, snake shoes for $150 a pair, in-the-velvet deer horns for $25 a pound, and pet ocelots and peregrine falcons selling for thousands and even hundreds of thousands of dollars. Illegally imported ivory and illegally taken big-game trophies bring big money. Deer, fish, small-game species and all kinds of birds—when channeled through the right market—mean big profits to the wildlife outlaw who is out after the quick, big buck.

The wildlife outlaw is a more serious violator than the first-time-out duck hunter who fails to sign his duck stamp. And he is not the same as the over-eager goose hunter who is suddenly overwhelmed by, and might shoot at, an after-sunset pair of Canada geese landing in his decoys. The guy who lies awake at night figuring a new way to beat the game warden, or make some quick cash at the expense of our precious wildlife, is not the average fish or game violator. He is a premeditative violator.

"You can't put everyone in the same basket." After almost thirty years of carrying the badge of a wildlife officer, I find Bill Waggoner's words about people and violators just as meaningful today as I did when he first handed me my badge and sent me north into the wilderness country. A good wildlife officer very quickly learns to size up the fish or game violator. He soon learns who are the hardcore outlaws.

The wildlife outlaw becomes an expert at his trade. This comes with practice. He plans his escape when he plans his violation. Often he does get away. This is not unusual.

He has many advantages on his side. He usually has a fast boat or car. His guns are usually expensive, and he spares little cost in the purchase of special nets, traps, night lights, and all kinds of specialized, custom-made equipment to help him get what he wants from the vulnerable outdoors.

He usually commits his acts against wildlife when animals are most vulnerable: when fish are spawning, when deer are blinded by lights, when waterfowl are enticed to the gun by bait. The outlaw manipulates the odds in his favor with the use of all kinds of illegal schemes. Only someone lying awake at night could dream them up.

Because of years of experience, the outlaw usually knows the lay of the land better than anyone else. He knows all the possible escape routes. He knows where the water is deep, where the river is shallow, where the tide runs out first, and where he can run, hide, or stash away any incriminating evidence. This evidence can be guns, lights, spears, bait, nets, traps, knives, or the fish or game he has illegally taken from the wild.

I have caught some wildlife outlaws in possession of some pretty sophisticated poaching gear. I have arrested wildlife outlaws with special night telescopic sights and silencers attached to their high-powered rifles. Crossbows, arrows that could be shot in a shotgun, and a telephone shocker used to kill trout in a well stocked stream, are just a few of the devices I have caught outlaws using.

I have found their guns hidden under the dashboard of their Cadillac and once found a rifle mounted under the running board of a bus.

I have apprehended waterfowl outlaws shooting ducks under power, noiselessly, as they moved up quickly on unsuspecting ducks in their camouflaged boat with an electric motor. I have arrested outlaws in scuba gear stealing lobsters from fishermen's legal traps. And I have often wondered about the good some of these clever outlaws could do if they put their talents toward some worthwhile wildlife cause.

But wildlife outlaws have more going for them in their illegal operations and escapes than just good equipment and familiarity with the terrain. Their lifetime experience helps a great deal when the warden gets close. The wildlife outlaw usually knows whom to trust and whom to avoid. The smart outlaw does his homework. He knows what kind of car the warden drives, where the warden lives, and checks up on the officer's comings and goings. He can spot "warden type" cars with or without state seals painted across the doors. The smart outlaw also knows that some states put their officers on schedules. They make it a point to learn those schedules and act accordingly.

Some states, thankfully not very many, require their officers to be always in full uniform; this makes covert or unannounced arrivals all but impossible. It's also hard to believe that a few states do not authorize their officers to carry firearms. This seems strange when almost everyone they come across during a hunting season carries a gun or weapon of some kind. You might think restrictions such as these were devised by the wildlife outlaws themselves.

Certain regulations seem to be written so carefully to protect the innocent that the guilty are almost impossible to convict. Such "loophole" laws are put on the books because of pressure from certain sportsmen's groups who are afraid that their members or associates may be curtailed to some extent in the way they hunt or fish. Unless well thought out and carefully written, regulations can end up protecting only those certain few. The resource and the public end up the losers.

Outlaws relish a regulation that has three or four excuses or "outs" built into it. A good officer is hoping only for a law or regulation which is enforceable. He knows no law is perfect.

The outlaw does get away—from state wardens and federal agents. This happens because of weather, mud, darkness, officer mistakes, crafty defense lawyers, judges' attitudes, or because the outlaw gets help from lookouts. Sometimes other "sportsmen" feel sorry for the almost caught outlaw, so they help him get away. Sometimes the press prints only one side of the story because the officer is not at liberty to tell his side until the trial. And like it or not, politicians sometimes get into the act to protect their constituents.

But by far the most effective way the wildlife outlaw gets away is to run. Let me tell you about a few frustrating times when outlaws ran away from me. Then I can tell you some better times when they didn't get away.

Over the ditch and through the woods

Running comes naturally. What do small boys do when they get caught throwing snowballs at the girls? They run. What do teenagers do when the farmer comes as they are about to take off with some of his pumpkins or apples? They run. What do nighttime fish and game outlaws do when the warden comes on the scene? They run too.

Wardens are not at all surprised when the wildlife outlaw runs off into the dark. In fact, they expect it. And besides, the outlaw runs because he has found that many times it works.

Veteran warden Bob Ward and I were after a known outlaw by the name of Red Hunter. We knew where and when he shined deer, what kind of gun he used, and what kind of car he drove.

Bob knew his job. He had been after Red for some time. I was still trying to learn the ropes. Bob had information that this was the time and the place to catch Red. Red was rumored to have killed about two hundred deer each year.

We were parked on the old Indian Creek road at the junction of two dead-end roads. One road went down to Indian Creek and died. The other went by some clover fields and then petered off into a dead-end too. There were no houses on either road.

I hid my car on a little stub road just a few feet from the junction. The clover fields were within sight. If a car came down past us and shined the fields, I would block the shiners as they returned past our corner. Even with my lack of experience, I didn't like the wide blocking point. There was too much road to cover with my car. I would have to rely on the fact that I could ease the other car off the road if Red and his pals wouldn't stop for the flashing red light. We would take that hurdle when we came to it.

We had driven down to the fields and had seen several deer feeding on the back end of the clover. They didn't seem concerned with our presence. Red had probably heard that the deer in these fields were pretty tame. Easy meat for a pro.

Once I had parked my new six-cylinder Chevy and covered it with my dyed black parachute, I brushed out my telltale tracks with a pine bough. Bob and I settled down to wait. Bob never ran out of stories, and I always looked forward to working with him and hearing more of his past exploits. He was also a joke teller.

I had just poured us a cup of coffee and was about to take a sip when I saw a light bobbing toward us. It was about ten o'clock and the moon was just breaking through the clouds over the fields below us.

Soon a car passed us and drove on toward the clover fields. The car stopped. A light swung out across the first field. The light had probably picked up the glistening green eyes of the two deer still feeding in the field. A shot rang out. "High-powered rifle," Bob said calmly. Then another shot. That usually meant "down with one, dead with two," but you never know.

The car spun its wheels. Without picking up a deer or going out into the field, and I felt sure, without dropping off anyone, it roared back toward our position. It was now picking up more speed. I was into my car as fast as I could go. Bob had cleared the brush and parachute from the front of my car and was on his way down the road ditch toward the oncoming car. "I'll come in from behind," he called over his shoulder.

I would pull out and be ready to block the car's path just before it hit the crossroads. Bob would lie in the ditch until the car reached his position. As the car went by, Bob would spring up and run behind it. As I pulled out and made the block and the shiner hit his brakes, Bob would come in fast on the passenger side of the outlaw car, placing its occupants under arrest before they could throw anything or attempt to run. Sound dangerous? It was.

My apprehensions were right. As I threw on my lights, siren, and drove out into the oncoming car's path, it slowed and then swerved hard to the right. I thought I might use my spotlight in the driver's eyes, but decided I had enough to handle. My real concern now was, did Bob get out of the ditch in time? Was he coming behind the car, or was he under it?

I couldn't stop now. I turned toward the oncoming lights and forced them further and further into the ditch. I expected to feel an impact any second. To my astonishment there was no collision. The shiner's car tore down into the ditch, up into the woods, tearing out or bending over three- to four-inch trees that were in its path.

As I rammed my car into reverse to turn around, the shiner car ripped through the woods parallel to the ditch, leaped the ditch, bounded like a drunken greyhound, and shot off down the road, throwing dust all over my car. By the time I got turned around, Bob was in my passenger door.

I spun my wheels as I asked the Chevy six for all it could muster. I wish it had the eight cylinders it appeared our adversary had. The fleeing shiner had about two miles to go to get back to the blacktop road.

The dust was filling my night world. I couldn't see the car taillights or the road ahead of me. I did know the road was pretty straight and that it came to a tee at the blacktop. As we hit the blacktop, we could see taillights disappearing over the hill to the west. I never got any closer. We didn't see the fleeing car again. After a few miles of fruitless driving, Bob said, "Let's go back."

We drove back to the scene of the shooting. We found where the shiner's car had stopped at the field. After a diligent search, we found one 30.06 cartridge that was still warm. This meant we were looking for a bolt action rifle, like the one Red Hunter was known to carry. The second casing was probably still in the gun. We found no downed deer, no blood, and no evidence that our shooter had hit home. Once you've heard it, you know when the bullet slams into a deer at night. We hadn't heard that sound.

We drove to where the shiners had gone around my road block. It looked like a bulldozer had run off the road for a hundred feet. There were ten to twelve trees leveled, several broken off. One was about four inches in diameter. The fleeing car, when it slammed back down on the road, must have broken a spring. The vehicle had hurtled through the air for over ten feet and Bob said he had heard something snap.

Bob had gotten part of a license plate number, but we didn't have enough to pin down a driver. We returned to the ditches beyond the "landing site."

"Here it is." Bob found a 30.06 in the ditch about 100 yards from the blocking point. It was a bolt action Springfield like the one Red was reported to use. It had a fired casing in the chamber and several more rounds in the magazine.

Bob and I finished up at the scene and drove to Red Hunter's house in the country. There was no car in the driveway or the yard. There was no activity in the house. It was almost 3 A.M. We stayed until 5 A.M., but nothing stirred. Our shiner had gotten away.

We found out later that our shiner had indeed been Red Hunter. He drove a Chevy just like mine, but his was a souped-up eight. Red did break a spring when he hit the road flying over the ditch. But Red was a pro. He didn't go home that night. Instead, he went to a friend's body shop and spent the rest of the night fixing his car.

We never did catch Red Hunter. But he did stop shining deer a couple of years later. He jumped another ditch, after battling a little too much alcohol in his *own* radiator. He hit another tree. But this time the tree was four feet in diameter, and the Chevy stopped dead. So did Red.

Another door

The sheriff needed help. He had a warrant for a young man who had been in trouble all of his life. He was wanted now for larceny in one of the big cities. The word was out that Joey had come back to his old village and was staying with one of his former girl friends. She lived in a tarpaper shack near the river. Joey was known for his ability to escape just when the law was about to apprehend him. He knew how and when to run.

Another warden and I had volunteered to help bring in Joey. Wardens in the north usually carried deputy sheriff credentials and often helped out the sheriff, just as the sheriff often helped wardens. There were so few law-enforcement officers in the north country that if we didn't work together, we were in deep trouble.

The other warden and the sheriff went to the front door of the shack just about dusk. I had carefully slipped back into the woods near the back door to catch Joey, should he decide to run out and disappear into the woods. That was one of his old tricks.

The sheriff signaled me with his flashlight. We were going in by the front door.

"This is the sheriff. Joey Bearbroke, come out with your hands up. I have a warrant for your arrest."

The plan was to give Joey a chance to come out. If he didn't appear in three minutes, the sheriff was going to go in, even if the door had to be pushed in. When the sheriff announced his arrival, we could hear some shuffling going on inside. Then we heard something break or tear. But Joey didn't come out through the front door, and there was no sign of his coming out by the back.

The sheriff had waited long enough. He and the other warden pushed open the front door and charged into the shack. Just then I heard some running noises over on the other side of the shack. Someone was crashing out through the woods into the dark.

I ran around the back of the shack and heard someone going off through the woods. Whoever he was, he had a good start. I looked back at the side of the shack. The sheriff was standing in a new opening in the wall. Joey had run right out through the wall, making a new door. We didn't find Joey.

Run, but watch where you run

Running away doesn't always work. Charlie was a well-known game law violator. He was the only person I knew who had been sent to the state prison on a charge of being a habitual game law violator. He had just gotten out when I first met him.

I met him one dark night as I blocked a shining car head-on. We were next to a field loaded with deer. We heard a shot, but couldn't hide the car and wait. We decided to just move in on the car as it shined the field.

As I hit my red light and siren, my partner jumped out and ran for the other car. Before my partner could get to the passenger side of the car, a man leaped from his car and ran into the woods carrying his 30-30 rifle. The escapee screamed and ran as if wild dogs were chasing him. He ran so fast he didn't look where he was going. He ran right into an eight-inch pine tree. The tree knocked the man backward to the ground, stunning him.

When Charlie came to, we stood over him, our flashlights in his eyes. All Charlie said was, "Please don't take my gun again." I apprehended Charlie two more times after the pine tree incident. It was a habit he couldn't seem to break.

How deep is the water?

Longtime violators engrossed in illegal wildlife operations always have lookouts. The lookout is someone who is just as interested in stealing from the wilderness as the active outlaw, but he is too old to run, too young to prosecute (thus "safe"), too fat or lazy to work at violating, or too drunk to hold a spear or a gun. Having a lookout often works.

For three years, I had been trying to catch some local boys (in their thirties) who speared the shoreline of Ripley Lake each spring. This time I was going to be there on the right night.

I had located their boat in the trees along the shoreline. The boat had been prepared during the day for that night's use. A spear handle was under the boat and gunnysacks placed next to the handle. The outlaws would bring their underwater light and spearhead with them when they arrived after dark.

I dropped Jim, one of my deputies, near the boat before dark. I had to take out my car via the dead-end road since there was no place to hide it. When I arrived back on foot at the boat area with another deputy, Jim told us a car had arrived. Two men took the boat and were out on the lake, and the driver had parked the car down at the boat landing. He appeared to be the lookout.

I decided to let the outlaws do their thing. If they did what they had done for years, they would spear the entire shoreline of the lake and take all the big walleyes they could put in their freezers for the year.

It was a bad night to move around. It was very dry and very hard to walk without stepping on twigs or dry leaves. I could hear the two men in the boat talking and occasionally bumping the boat. With my binoculars I could see one standing on the back seat holding a spear handle. The other man was rowing the boat backwards. I couldn't see a light, but I knew their underwater light would show up very little onshore.

We crept carefully back to the road and moved quietly around the boat landing and the lookout. We hoped to get on the other side of the lookout and grab his friends before they finished spearing the shoreline back at their car.

I could see the fishermen on the lake were having some success, pulling up a fish every now and then on the end of their spear. After an hour and a half, the spearers had come almost around the lake. They would be just about in front of us soon.

I had not picked a very good place. The water here was of a depth unknown to me and my partners. I could see us charging out into ten feet of water shouting, "Conservation Wardens, you're under arrest," as the three of us sank to the bottom and the boat rowed leisurely away.

At the last minute I decided to move farther back toward the lookout, where I knew the water was shallower. That was my big mistake.

Suddenly the dim light we had been watching went out. I could see the boat start to move faster out onto the lake. Soon the boat was so far out I couldn't see it anymore. They had been spooked. The lookout had somehow discovered us and, probably with a prearranged signal, warned his partners someone was on the shore waiting for them.

After we lost track of the boat for about half an hour, we went to the landing and arrested the lookout just as he was about to drive off. The boat had disappeared. The lookout claimed he knew nothing about illegal fishing activities on the lake. He just liked to sit alone on the shore in his car and "think about things."

We found the boat the next morning on the far shore. It still had a car battery, an underwater light, and a spear handle in it. It also had about an inch of fish scales on its bottom. Our spearers had carried off their bags of fish through the woods to their freezers.

I later prosecuted the lookout as an accomplice. He was found guilty, appealed, was found guilty again, and paid a $50 fine. I'm sure he received his share of the fish, which belonged to the public, for the inconvenience of having to go to court.

Too quiet night

Each spring, the state put big nets into the lake on which I lived to spawn muskies. The nets were scattered in four locations on the lake. Fish of all kinds would get into these nets each night. The biologists would come the next morning to spawn and release the muskies and turn all the fish back into the cold, clear water.

Gus called me early in the afternoon. He ran a tavern on the shore of the lake. Gus cared about the lake and its fish.

"Three young men were in drinking beer this morning. They were talking about trying to break into the nets from a canoe. They said they just about tipped over, but would go back tonight with a big boat and clean out the nets."

I lined up all the help I could for that night to watch all the nets. I had wardens and other fishery personnel stationed at vantage points where they could guard all the nets. We even covered the lakeshore home of one of the suspected culprits. We knew he was capable of doing what Gus had described.

The hours went by. Nothing happened. It was now after midnight. My helpers started to get restless. There was a big fisheries meeting the next day at the state capital and most of my helpers had to leave early in the morning to get to the meeting. Soon everyone had left, except for two fellow wardens from adjacent counties who had come over to give me a hand. They guarded the nets on the far shore. I "sat on" the nets on the town side of the lake.

It was now 2 A.M. and I heard a car coming down the landing road. I had parked my car back in the brush about seventy-five yards from the landing. Three men got out, put in a boat, and rowed toward the muskie nets out near the island. One man stayed in the car. He was the lookout.

I watched with my glasses as the boat moved quietly toward the net. I couldn't see the boat after it got beyond the island. I knew what they were up to. I sure wished I had all my helpers in position now. I decided I would have to get more help.

It was deathly silent, and I hated to use my radio. In those days when we transmitted, a loud dynamotor in the radio would whine. The noise *could* be heard by an alert lookout. I had to chance it. I pressed the mike button, and called the two wardens on the other side of the lake.

"Come over and walk in to where I am. The poachers are now out into the nets."

The lookout was alert. He must have heard the noise and somehow signaled his friends. They landed at another part of the lake. By the time we rounded up the suspects and questioned them, they were clean. (They had even showered.) We found the stolen boat later, full of fish scales and blood. The outlaws all got away.

"Me Englash she not so good."

Our agents had good information that Massachusetts fur dealers, who owned a big warehouse near the waterfront in Boston, would be bringing in a load of illegal fisher fur from New Hampshire tonight. We had New Hampshire officers, Massachusetts officers, and federal agents waiting for them when they arrived at their warehouse at 11 P.M. I was in my nearby office, helping to coordinate the raid by radio.

Once the wildlife officers were in the warehouse, I left my office and drove to the darkened street, which was the site of several warehouses and run-down vacant buildings. As the fur dealers started to unload their fur into the warehouse, the officers moved in for the arrest. To our surprise, there were no illegal fisher pelts in the truck.

The fur dealers spoke Italian and very little English. We still felt there were illegal pelts in the warehouse and, somehow overcoming the language barrier, gained consent from the owners to look through the warehouse. The fur dealers were very cooperative. They escorted the officers throughout the four-story warehouse, shining flashlights into all the rooms and storage spaces.

Some untagged fur was located, but due to the weak tagging laws of Massachusetts, no seizures could be made. We didn't find any illegal fisher pelts. We went away with a permit violation; it turned out to be partially the fault of the issuing agent, so no action was taken.

About a year later, these same fur dealers were better known to us. One of our agents, in an undercover capacity, found out what really happened the night of the warehouse raid.

He found out why the fisher pelts we expected to find didn't get into the fur dealer's truck. The New Hampshire outlaw trapper they were to buy them from couldn't be contacted by the fur dealers. The trapper hadn't paid his phone bill and his phone was disconnected on the day the pickup was to be made.

The undercover agent also found out that the Italian fur dealers really spoke better English than they let on. Their excuse that the lights didn't work on all the floors of their warehouse was just another way to keep us from seeing as well as we would have liked.

While we were downstairs trying to get through the language barrier, one of the employees was upstairs piling illegal untagged fur into a heap. With the help of an electric forklift, he was covering the illegal fur with a large number of low-grade muskrat pelts that no officer would be interested in. The night of the warehouse fur raid was not one of our better nights. The outlaws got away.

How he gets caught

Catching the real wildlife outlaw is not the same as catching people who occasionally violate the fish and game laws. The wildlife officer seldom stumbles onto the serious premeditating violator in the midst of his well planned crime. To catch the outlaw, the officer needs help; and information is an important form of help. Going after the outlaw with only half a bag of information is like getting out on the basketball floor for a big game, wearing only one shoe.

Information can come from many sources. Calls even come from an irate neighbor or a "friend" of the violator who suddenly feels that he has been cheated. I have received reliable information from such sources as former accomplices, jealous women, relatives, fellow employees, and even angry wives.

Unfortunately, many well-meaning people consider the act of informing on even a serious wildlife outlaw as that of a snitch or stool pigeon. In fact, statistics show that serious wildlife violations committed right in front of other people are seldom reported. Added to the old-time snitch attitude is another antiquated idea that the fish and game belong to the government or the state; therefore, the citizen has no responsibility to wildlife and should not become involved.

More people are becoming involved. More people are beginning to feel that they have something at stake when their special wild places are jeopardized or when wildlife they have a personal interest in are threatened or destroyed. People are becoming less apt to turn away when a flagrant wildlife violation takes place before their eyes.

There are other lesser known ways that wildlife outlaws get caught. Sometimes an outlaw's conscience or fear of getting caught is his worst enemy. Drugs and alcohol and just plain greed make violators less cautious. Perseverence by a wildlife officer can be the key to putting an outlaw behind bars. And using specialized warden equipment—long range telescopes, night vision scopes, tape recorders, crime scene kits, special radios, metal detectors, and other investigative aids—a wildlife officer can cut down some of the escape advantages the outlaw often has. Recently, trained dogs have been used to catch the outlaw.

Freak happenings can also lead to the apprehension of the wildlife outlaw. It can be a sudden change in the weather. He runs out of gas, or his car won't start. His luck turns sour, or the warden's luck suddenly becomes overpowering—like going to the wrong house to search for a deer and finding the refrigerator full of illegal venison.

I'd like to tell you now about some informants, some unusual happenings, and some strange circumstances that sent wildlife outlaws to jail. Those who want to preserve their natural resources should be aware that giving information to a wildlife officer takes courage. Standing up for anything takes courage.

An angry woman

In an earlier chapter of this book, I told of a woman who angrily watched two men kill a doe in the field across the road from her farm. She had been watching the doe and her fawns feed in that field long enough to care about them. The woman felt strongly that she must do something. She did not feel that the deer belonged to the state or the government. She didn't wait for her husband to come home because she knew that might be too late. She became involved because she wanted to. She felt a responsibility.

Unfortunately, information reported by the average citizen—no matter how well-meaning—is quite worthless when it is late, skimpy, or inaccurate. Last summer's information is usually late (but not always). A nondescript person in a nondescript car, committing a wildlife crime, is not enough information for an officer to take action. If you really want to help protect the resource, your information must be something like the angry woman's.

Watching from her kitchen window, the farmer's wife grew more angry with each ticking minute. As she watched the two men in the act of killing "her" deer, she picked up her phone. Listen to the description she gave us of the car that the two doe shooters were driving:

Their car is parked right now fifty yards east of our mailbox. It is a 1952 faded blue or gray, somewhat rusted Plymouth or Chrysler. The car has a sun visor on it with a chrome rim around it. On the back it has black rubber mud flaps that run all the way along the back of the bumper. On the top they have a homemade top rack, made out of boards with rubber suction cups to hold it secure. They have a rusted spotlight on the driver's side, and it hangs down like it might be broken. It has a Wisconsin plate number, but I can only get the first letter and the first two numbers. They are H86 and three more numbers.

There was only one car in the world that could come close to matching the woman's description. In one day, with the help of the sheriff and state police, we located the car, matched up the tire tread to our plaster casts, and found deer hair on the rear floor where the woman said she had seen them load the deer.

Interrogation of the driver of the car gave us information on where the deer had been taken. Other wardens went to that farm immediately. The wardens arrived just in time to find the car driver's partner and his brother-in-law loading two illegal deer into their car. They had heard the driver had been arrested. The arrests happened solely because of the assistance from an honestly angry, but thinking and caring woman.

The lone ranger

Most of us believe what our background has trained us to believe. We rally to the tales of Robin Hood and his merry men poaching the king's deer and other game animals to feed the poor and less privileged folk. And through the years, public opinion has swung to the side of the poor, down-trodden, backwoods farmer who slips behind his desolate farm to shoot one of the state's numerous deer, just to feed his starving wife and seven children. Any game warden who would arrest or even interfere with such a survival operation certainly should be run out of town.

I have to admit there are a few farmers who do survival hunting. They poach wildlife just to feed the family—without selling deer, without infringing on their neighbors, and without taking much more game than their family can use. Chances are almost zero that the little old farmer will ever be discovered.

But the real poacher usually gets caught when his quiet "survival" hunt turns into something less palatable to game wardens and the public alike. Let me tell you about a man who was "just feeding the family."

Barney Jason was a crack shot. He talked about it to anyone who would listen.

"I can put a 30-30 slug between a deer's eyes, at night, from a car window, at a hundred yards before the car even comes to a stop." Barney liked to brag. He liked to build up his shooting eye and night-hunting courage with a few drinks from his favorite backwoods bar.

A young, newly married man, who lived on the edge of one of Barney's favorite shining fields, got tired of Barney's "feeding the family" antics. After a 30-30 slug ripped through the young man's back porch and embedded itself in a nearby pine, the young man gave me a call.

He said he had recognized Barney's car, not only that night, but many nights previously. He told me he would call the next time Barney shot a deer next to his house. He'd use the code name Lone Ranger.

The following Saturday night, a phone call came into the state police dispatcher. The young man on the phone said the Lone Ranger wanted me to come on the double. I was reached by radio since I was fifty miles away, watching another likely shining field.

At eighty miles per hour, red light flashing, I headed for the Lone Ranger's house. When I started on the back roads near his place, I slowed down and cut my lights. When I arrived at the field, the young man told me what I expected: "Barney's car has left, but I watched them shoot a deer and load it into Barney's car about an hour ago."

I had been told that Barney would be at one of three places: his hunting partner's house, skinning out the deer; the tavern, celebrating his success; or at home, a one-room shack where he, his wife, and six children lived.

By now I had help. I had a deputy with me, and by radio called in my neighboring warden and his deputy. We separated and headed to the two homes.

It was midnight by the time I reached Barney's shack. It was completely dark, with no activity. I received the same report from my fellow warden. There was a parked car with a cold radiator at the house of Barney's hunting partner. We headed for the tavern.

I saw the car that had been described to me as soon as I pulled up in front of the tavern. It was Barney's. Barney was not being very careful tonight. A quick look at the back bumper and trunk area showed fresh blood and deer hair. Flashing a light into the car, I saw the gun and a light on the back seat.

We went into the tavern. (We were in uniform.) There were twenty tough-looking men pushed up to the bar. The loud-talking, storytelling atmosphere was about to change as we stepped through the tavern door.

We knew we would have to take command of this place or the people in it would take command of us. One of our deputies went straight to the jukebox and pulled the plug. My fellow warden went right to the bartender so he could tell him why we were there. Our other deputy, a big man who weighed about 250 pounds, stood at the door, his badge pinned to the front of his coat. Suddenly, silence crashed in on the place as after a bomb has exploded.

I knew the reputation of this place; we had to be on the offense every minute. I stepped up toward the men at the bar and broke the silence.

"We want to talk to the owner of that black Ford with the fresh blood and hair on its bumper. It's parked out in front."

No one moved. No one spoke. I took a chance.

"Barney Jason here? The license checks out to Barney Jason."

I watched as several pairs of eyes turned toward a rough-looking man who stood at the end of the bar. He had a bottle of beer in his hand. I had a partial description of Barney Jason.

"You Barney Jason?"

"So what?" I grabbed him by the arm that held the bottle.

"You're under arrest, let's go outside."

I hustled Barney toward the door before he could take in what was happening. I took the bottle from his hand and set it on the bar on the way out. When I got Barney outside, I told him we wanted his partner.

My big deputy had followed me out. I told him to go back and tell Whitey Rocko we wanted him out here too. In one minute we were all outside with our two prisoners. I'm sure Whitey and the bar full of startled men thought Barney had told us about Whitey when, in fact, the Lone Ranger had.

We didn't wait around to congratulate ourselves about our success. One of the deputies drove Barney's car. Whitey was put in the other warden's car and Barney, hands cuffed behind his back, rode with me.

On the way to the sheriff's office, Barney, who was really feeling no pain, told me that he was a good shot. I encouraged him to tell me just how good he was. He said he had killed four deer in three nights, including the one he had in the trunk of his car. He shot them all on the move, through the car window, while Whitey held the light. He wouldn't say what he had done with the other three deer.

By the time we settled Barney and Whitey securely in their cells and completed our investigation, it was almost dawn. At about 7 A.M., I drove north to Barney's house to tell his wife where he had spent the night.

A very dirty, hungry-looking young boy came to the door when I knocked. I asked whether his mother was home. He called, "Ma, a policeman." A very tired-looking, gaunt woman came to the door. She looked like she was about fifty, but I believe she was only about thirty-five. I told her about her husband's escapade. She didn't look surprised. I couldn't help noticing the hungry look of the children and Mrs. Jason.

"Do you have enough to eat in this house?"

"We go to town for surplus foods tomorrow if Barney gets back to take us."

"What about the venison? Don't you get venison when your husband kills four deer in three nights, as he told me on the way to jail?"

"He sells those. Then he drinks away the money."

I was thinking, I'm sure Barney will decide to tell the court he killed the deer just to feed the family, and now I have seen the family.

I told the woman I would be back. That afternoon I returned with the welfare director. He brought four boxes of groceries. I brought a car-killed deer. I had paid $3 for the deer, and a friend at the supermarket had cut it up and wrapped it for nothing. I'm sure that what we brought was soon gone, but it was more food than that house had seen for a while.

Barney was convicted and sent to jail for ten days. Barney told the judge just what I thought he would about "just feeding the family." It was a tale that often caused the court to let the defendant get away. This time the judge didn't buy it; Barney went to jail.

The real answer to controlling the illegal taking of wildlife is in the hands of the people. By caring enough to do something about the serious fish and game law violators, we can encourage state and government wildlife agencies to pass sensible regulations and can back strict enforcement of those regulations.

Several western states and some eastern states have twenty-four-hour hot lines for citizens to report wildlife violations. These hot-line systems are backed up by a reward system in most cases, to encourage people to call the authorities to the scene. People are learning that it is their wilderness and their wildlife to protect. But we're learning slowly.

I feel the public does care. I have seen the difference in a courtroom, where interested organizations and citizens take the time to watch fish and game violation trials. Judges and juries seem to conduct themselves more responsibly when they know they have an audience of citizens who care. Don't we all?

The old off-with-the-raincoat trick

Even rookies run into the wildlife outlaw. It is hoped that when they do, no one gets hurt. If someone *has* to get hurt, let's hope it is the outlaw. In this story, he just gets wet.

After a year as a warden in the north country, I felt I was almost an old hand. Little did I know how much more I had to learn. It was spring—time to learn about fish runs and fish spearers.

A local informant had told me that some old-time fish spearers would be out tonight. They would be out to spear a boatload of northern pike on the Namekagon River, just upstream from the old Springbrook Bridge.

My trainee warden, Milt Diekman (now a veteran warden supervisor), and I arrived at the river just before dark. A steady rain had started. We parked our car about a mile from the bridge where we had to cross the river.

Our informant, who was much concerned over the continual slaughter of spawning fish on this river, told us in detail just where and when we would find the culprits.

"Just hike up the river about dark from the old bridge and along the path on the north side. You'll come to a huge pine tree in the middle of the path. Just beyond that there is an opening and a sand bar landing on the river. You'll find them in a boat, a car battery hooked to an underwater light. One man will be rowing the boat backwards and the other will be standing on the back seat spearing and bagging fish. They go every night when the fish are running. They'll have a lookout."

We hiked in the rain to get to the bridge. It was getting dark.

"Hold it," Milt said, "There are a couple of lookouts in a car parked right next to the path we have to follow."

We sat down and pondered how to get across the bridge and onto the path without being observed. After ten minutes of fading daylight and our growing frustration, a car suddenly roared away in a spray of gravel. Almost before the gravel had settled, Milt and I were across the bridge and hurrying up the path toward the landing. The rain continued.

As we crept quietly along the path, I heard a strange crunching sound behind me. When I stopped, the noise stopped. When I started, the noise started again. When I stopped, Milt stopped. It was Milt. It was his rattling raincoat.

"Milt, take off that noisy raincoat. They can hear you coming like a moose coming out of the dry brush."

Just then I found myself bumping into the big pine tree in the middle of the path. Milt slipped off his coat and we slid around the tree into the opening. I hoped that if our spearing friends were out in their boat, they hadn't heard Milt playing moose in his raincoat. I pulled out my binoculars to look out on the river. Just then we saw the boat, a dim light at its stern. With the binoculars I could make out two people in the boat, just as our informant had reported.

Milt and I started to whisper plans to snag the culprits as they hit shore with their illegal fish. Then my heart sank. Not more than thirty feet away, right in front of the landing, someone lit a match to a cigarette. Another lookout. Unbelievably, he hadn't heard us. Milt and I faded into the bush.

We quickly made our plan to jump all three as the boat touched the shore. We didn't have to wait long. Soon the underwater light went out and, with our light-gathering binoculars, we could see that the two men in their boat were headed right for us and our landing. Old Smokey with his cigarette made it easy for us to locate him.

The boat hit the shore. Milt and I hit the landing on the run, our flashlights suddenly glaring into the startled spearers' eyes.

"Conservation wardens," we announced. "You're under arrest."

The lookout started to run to my right, along the river. Not wanting to chase him and leave both boat operators to Milt, I pushed Old Smokey as hard as I could out into the shallow river. I turned just as one of the boat spearers tried to run by me toward the big pine. I took after him and made a tackle Lombardi would have been proud of before my spearer got to the path.

I slipped the cuffs onto my new friend's wrist and pulled him to his feet. Just as I looked around to see where Milt was, his big hand came down on my culprit's cuffed hands.

"I've got him." In his other hand, Milt had the other burly spearer by the back of his red wool shirt.

Milt knew I wanted to get back to Old Smokey, somewhere out in the cold, rolling Namekagon River. I shone my bright light out onto the river and there was our lookout standing up to his armpits in the springtime, forty-five-degree water. He gladly took my outstretched hand.

Milt and I cuffed Smokey and his red-coated spearing friend together. We gathered up the light, battery, and spear and loaded the big sack of fish—some weighing over ten pounds apiece—over the shoulder of one of our culprits. We headed for the bridge. It continued to rain.

As we approached the bridge, I could see the lookouts were back, parked where they had been before. We kept going. I hoped the car occupants would figure it was just their spear-toting friends returning from a successful fish-taking adventure.

As we got near the car, I hurried on ahead while Milt herded our soggy crew up the path. I reached the car window on the driver's side.

"Conservation wardens." To my surprise I saw a light and a spear in the back seat. "You're under arrest."

The lookouts had a bag of fish in the trunk. It seems the greedy young men got bored and decided to drive home to get their own spear for a few fish of their own. Their greed worked in our favor. It gave Milt and me a chance to cross the bridge and (minus a rattling raincoat) slip up to the boat landing at just the right time.

The judge found all the spearers guilty. He fined the two boatmen and Old Smokey a total of $175 (a lot of money for that country in those days). The two undependable lookout spearers paid $10 each. (They were only eighteen.) No one lost his fishing license. Milt lost his noisy raincoat. The community lost sixty-two pounds of spawning northerns from the Namekagon, today classified as a wilderness river. But our informant knew he had done what he could to protect the river he loved. He could sleep a little easier.

"*There ain't no warden in a hundred miles.*"

I didn't dare breathe. The deer shiners' car was ten feet from me. I had turned my portable two-way radio off just in case it might disrupt the ongoing night scene with a blat, a squelch noise, or a nearby warden call. I was in the road ditch lying flat on my face.

Just two minutes before, the old car and its three occupants had roared up into the trap we had set for them. The young men in the car were the right ones. They were in their early twenties, but quite experienced at killing deer at night and evading the local game warden. They certainly matched our information.

I knew they were experienced, as I watched them shine and shoot a doe in seconds. They killed the deer in the field directly across from my stakeout point. Their car had not even stopped before the light hit the deer full in the eyes. In one quick shot they dropped the deer. The bullet caught her in the left temple.

I had been watching the deer in those fields for about an hour. It had been raining off and on with a full moon blowing in and out of the clouds. I had been keeping dry in an old shed just off the road behind me.

After four hours of waiting and watching, I heard warden Cliff Freeman on the radio. He reported a suspicious car moving along our road (about two miles east of me). Cliff said the car went into the field near him, but he heard no shot. He said something was being loaded into the trunk.

Next, the car's lights came bobbing toward me. I knew wardens could have every road in this five-mile area blocked in about two minutes. We were ready. We seldom had this much manpower in one place.

The deer killers we were after had been shooting deer in this area for over two months. The local warden, after receiving several calls from nearby residents and having no success in apprehending the violators, called for help. Four cars and ten wardens came from seven counties to saturate the area. Now it was about to pay off.

Before I turned off my radio, I alerted the warden in the car two miles to the west of me that I had just observed the night hunters shoot the deer. Warden cars began to block off the road the outlaws and I were on.

I lifted my head to see the driver step out of his car, wearing a green baseball cap. Holding a spotlight on the downed deer, he said, "Hurry up and get that goddamn thing into the car!" The two other parties—a tall, lean, bearded man of about twenty-five and his short, fat, brown-jacketed partner—ran toward the deer. The tall, bearded one shouted back over his shoulder, "Don't worry, there ain't no goddamn game warden in a hundred miles of here."

I felt like jumping up and saying, "The hell there isn't." But instead, I watched as the two rough-looking men carried and dragged the dead deer back to the road. They threw the limp animal into the trunk and jumped into the back seat. "Let's get another one," I heard the driver whoop as he threw the still running car into gear and tore gravel, sending it flying in all directions. I got on the radio.

I knew there was only one chance that the deer shiners would turn around and head back the way they came. There was a little turn-around road just one hundred yards west of me. Once the outlaw car sped by the turn-around, I knew they would keep going west on the narrow road until they hit an intersection two miles away.

"C–117 to C–125," I radioed. "They're on their way west and they're driving a dark brown Ford. There are three men in the car. The tall, bearded one shot the deer. The driver held the light. The short, fat one helped drag the deer and put it in the trunk."

I knew there would be two cars blocking the road and greeting our friends when they got to the intersection. But local warden Manthie wanted to be sure. I heard him call, "Clear the road, I'm coming in behind them." I was now standing on the road watching the outlaws' taillights disappear in the west. Then I heard Ed's car coming fast. I stepped off the road just as Ed tore by with his lights out.

As the outlaws' car arrived at the intersection, their world fell in on them. Red lights, headlights, and sirens hit them from three directions. As they came to a screeching stop, wardens on foot came in on all doors, placing them under arrest with flashlights blazing into their astonished faces. I identified the deer killers at the scene.

The courts in Rusk County were tough on deer shiners. Each man received the maximum $200 fine and 10 days in jail; they lost their new rifle, and their car went on the auction block several months later. They don't all get away.

William

Any violator who is out to make money from our nation's wildlife has earned the right to be called a wildlife outlaw. My years of experience have taught me that this robber does cause real harm to our jeopardized wildlife populations.

I believe the most effective tool that state and federal wildlife agencies can use to combat the illegal wildlife commercializer is the same tool used by the drug enforcement agencies: undercover operations.

William was a special agent of the U.S. Fish and Wildlife Service. To the owners and operators of the Shady Brook Farm and Country Store on the outskirts of Boston, William (or Willy) appeared to be an easygoing, somewhat disreputable, often unemployed outdoorsman. For a few bucks, he could furnish a deer or two that could be resold for big bucks across the counter of the country store.

The store made its $5- to $10-per-pound sales of venison under the guise of legal deer meat coming from licensed game farms that raised deer behind fences. In reality, the store hadn't purchased a game farm deer for several years, but sold two to three hundred deer every year over its counters. The deer came from all kinds of sources—none of them legal—sources such as illegal hunters and poachers from many parts of the state and surrounding area.

William had approached the country store in an undercover capacity because he had heard from a reliable source that the Shady Brook Farm and Country Store "sure seemed to be doing a big business in game farm deer sales." After checking some of the known legal game farms, he knew that the Shady Brook deer had to be coming from somewhere besides a game farm.

After William made several trips to the country store, the operators began to accept him. After checking out his car license plate and calling the New Hampshire surveying company Willy claimed he worked for parttime, the Shady Brook people were ready to do business. But Willy had to be always on his guard. He lived only a mile from the country store.

As the months rolled by and the fall season came on, deer sales at the store must have been on the increase. Leo the butcher was apparently very much involved in the illegal purchase and sale of deer and geese. One day he asked Willy if he could furnish a larger number of deer, as the holiday season was coming on. (Deer prices could rise drastically during the holiday season.) Shortly after that, the owners approached Willy and asked him if he could bring in a "good supply" of venison. Willy told them he would see what he could do.

The next time Willy brought a deer to the store he was paid $159 for it; the deer weighed 159 pounds.

"I can get you ten more deer," Willy told Leo, "but you'll have to go to New Hampshire to pick them up."

He told the owners and Leo that bringing illegal deer across the state line from New Hampshire was a federal offense, a violation of the Lacey Act. All three agreed that only meant that everyone, including Willy, would have to be very careful.

Willy told Leo they could pick up the ten deer the following weekend at the home of a friend. The deer would be stored in the friend's garage. The following weekend, Leo drove the Shady Brook Farm truck to New Hampshire. Willy rode along and showed Leo the way.

They backed up to a garage on the outskirts of a little New Hampshire town. There they were met by a man named Tom. Tom sold them ten deer, which they loaded into the truck. Tom was paid $420 in cash for the ten deer. Leo told Tom he would take all the deer that Tom could deliver. Tom said he would see what he could do.

The deer in the back of the closed suburban truck were deer that the state had confiscated from other illegal hunters. Tom watched as Willy and Leo drove away, headed for the barn at the Shady Brook Farm and Country Store. Tom was a federal agent. A New Hampshire state officer took pictures of the sale from the trunk of a car across the street.

An undercover operation lasting about two years led to the raid one Saturday morning by a combined state-federal unit that seized this venison and other illegal game parts. After trial, owners and operators later paid large fines and were put on probation.

The next day, with both state and federal search warrants, special agents and Massachusetts officers raided the Shady Brook Farm and Country Store. Besides the ten deer, a truckload of other illegal venison was seized, plus some Canada geese that Leo had there for sale. Leo had told Willy how easy it was "to bait the geese in down by the river," and then "snag them by baiting a fishhook with corn." Leo said the meat was never damaged this way and he could get $15 to $20 per bird around holiday time.

The owners and operators of the country store were charged with conspiracy in New Hampshire federal court. They paid large fines and were put on probation. The country store was soon sold. It no longer sells wildlife; it's now a fruit market. William is still Willy, in another part of the country.

Deer Week II

The November 1976 issue of *Country Journal* magazine contained an article entitled "Deer Week." The author of the article, Jeff Wheelwright (New York freelance writer), described how he met a Billy Cooper in a western Massachusetts bar called Henry's Club. He seemed to become enraptured by the lifestyle of Billy Cooper, his family and friends. The writer stated that Billy Cooper wasn't the man's real name and told in great detail, almost with reverence, the many exploits of Billy Cooper and friends.

He told how Henry's Club was the scene of "expected" Saturday night fights and punch-outs among the patrons, men and women alike. But most importantly, the freelance writer wrote about Billy's mad passion for hunting deer, legal and otherwise. Billy's hunting partners were described in detail and the gang's disregard for the wildlife laws were written off with:

> Although Billy is an outlaw according to the fish and game laws, few country people fully obey those laws themselves. Like Billy, they tend to see hunting and fishing restrictions as interference from Boston bureaucrats and environmentalists with their traditional rights.

The writer reported the gang's deer week escapades, which included shooting from vehicles, killing does illegally, failing to tag the deer they killed, killing over the limit, hunting during closed season and after legal hours, and hunting on posted private property. The writer also stated his reaction to Billy Cooper's hunting methods and attitudes toward game laws:

> I had heard that Billy and his gang of outlaws had taken six deer off my land last year, running them down over my hill, shooting them one by one, and loading them in trucks parked right in my driveway. I also heard he had every intention of doing it again this year. Safer, I decided at last, to join him than fight him. A week before the opening of the season, I went to his [Billy's] bakery to ask him to take me hunting.

Step by step, the writer led the reader along as he hunted with Billy Cooper and his outlaw partners, shooting at whatever moved in the woods and flagrantly violating every legal and moral code in the books. The local natural resource officer was treated in the article as if he were easily fooled, as if he thought Billy Cooper was little more than a "friendly outlaw."

Billy and his gang of deer hunting outlaws really did exist. And they hunted just as the magazine writer described. The names used in the article were not their real names, but their disregard for wildlife and wildlife laws *was* real.

The article drew some hot retorts in the next few issues of *Country Journal* via the "letters to the editor" section. Here's what a few people had to say about "Deer Week":

From New Hampshire—"Your November issue of *Country Journal* contains an article by Jeff Wheelwright, 'Deer Week,' which you no doubt feel is entertaining reading, I find the article disgusting. I realize that my likes and dislikes are not shared by all the readers of *Country Journal*; however, I do believe there is a large percentage of your readers who feel like I do."

From Vermont—"I just finished reading 'Deer Week' in your November issue, and the more I read the more I despised Billy Cooper. This article makes him out to be some sort of a hero that you should admire like Billy the Kid. Mr. Cooper thinks of himself as lord and master of the deer around him, ignoring rules and regulations like a spoiled child. His attitude toward the no trespassing signs certainly wouldn't be tolerated around here. It's a good thing everyone doesn't think like Billy Cooper, or the Billy Cooper who likes to 'look at the deer too' and takes his kids out to 'watch them in the summer,' may not have anything to show his grandchildren."

And finally from Pennsylvania—"Billy Cooper is certainly a real man. He gets into brawls in the local bar. He leads men deer hunting, paramilitary style. He has little respect for others' property rights. He disregards game laws. He does these things because, 'he needs the freedom of movement and spirit that hunting provides.' Our hero, his mental facilities apparently equal to his trigger finger, 'is quick to see double standards of justice.'

"Billy Cooper emerges as this: a frustrated person who is unable to react rationally to the forces in his life. Anyone whose sole purpose in life (other than providing for his family) is hunting is not healthy. Perhaps Billy Cooper becomes a symbol. But, my God, he's not worthy of being a hero. And Jeff Wheelwright has tried to make him a folk hero. I see no admirable characteristics in Billy Cooper. Whenever I feel myself, perhaps inevitably, returning to some neolithic times, I will try to remember Billy Cooper and that he is everything I don't want to be."

The readers of *Country Journal* were not the only people who were distressed by the antics of Billy Cooper and his gang. Natural resource officers from Massachusetts had already begun to investigate Mr. Cooper and his friends. Because some of the illegal deer the gang was taking were hauled across the state line into Connecticut—in violation of the

Lacey Act—we, as federal agents, were asked to assist the state. Working with both Connecticut and Massachusetts officers, two special agents became involved with Billy Cooper and his "folk hero deer hunting ventures."

For two years, during two deer weeks, the agents joined Billy Cooper's gang of outlaws. Everything in the magazine article was true. After the second season had come to a close, Billy and his hunting companions had a surprise visit, at Billy's home.

They were having a little drinking celebration in the living room, after hiding three of their untagged deer in a barn, then scaring the neighbors by shooting their high-powered rifles behind the house after dark. Suddenly three vehicles arrived; two drove into the driveway.

Uniformed Massachusetts and Connecticut officers and federal agents surrounded the house. A third vehicle with more officers parked on the road at the entrance to the driveway, protecting the officers from any Cooper gang arrivals. A Massachusetts supervisor, Ed Lawler, and federal agent Clyde Bolin rapped on the door, armed with arrest and search warrants straight from the judge's desk.

We took all of Billy Cooper's gang out of the house, one by one, cuffed them and transported them to the county jail.

Billy Cooper was charged in Massachusetts state court with shooting a doe without a permit, failing to tag deer, failing to report a kill, shooting from a truck, shooting while within 500 feet of a house, having a loaded gun in a motor vehicle, shooting more than one deer, and continuing to hunt after shooting a deer. He pleaded guilty to killing an anterless deer without a permit and paid $1,250 in state fines. Eight other charges were dropped.

Henry and Richard, the father and son from Connecticut, who were described in the article as having identical black mustaches and long hair, paid $937.50 and $375.00 for aiding in the transportation of an illegal deer. Several other charges were dropped. Donny, Billy's nephew, paid $125.00 for aiding in the transportation of an illegal deer. Francis, who had come back from Florida for deer week, paid $249.50 for false application to obtain a license, failure to report a deer kill within 24 hours, hunting with an invalid license, and failure to tag a deer. Close to $5,000 was paid in state court by the gang. All defendants received a mandatory loss of Massachusetts hunting privileges for one year; the deer were seized by the state.

But it wasn't over for Billy Cooper or Henry, Richard, and several others who participated in the previous season's hunt. They were charged in federal court under the Lacey Act for transporting illegally taken deer across state lines. They paid civil penalties for those violations.

Billy Cooper paid a $500 civil penalty. He was also ordered to perform 64 hours of service for the Massachusetts Fish and Game Department.

The undercover operations were conducted with utmost secrecy and care. Very few people knew that special agents were part of Billy Cooper's gang for two hunting seasons. In fact, I received a letter of request from one of the Massachusetts commissioners, who had read the *Country Journal* article. His officers were the ones attempting to apprehend Billy's gang. The letter request was for our agency to assist the state in an undercover operation to bring the Cooper gang to court. I was pleased to call the commissioner that same day.

"We move fast." I said coyly, "We already have your suspects in jail." I then told him about Deer Week II.

Oh, by the way—Billy Cooper's sixty-four hours of state service for the Fish and Game Department were spent building bluebird houses. Deer Week II is the real story. They don't all get away.

PART V

THE WILDLIFE OFFICER

Who is he?

Thirty years have taught me that the average American knows little about wildlife and even less about wildlife officers. This is not unusual considering the fact that, with few exceptions, our educational process includes very little teaching about wildlife. And how many people, young or old, have ever seen a wildlife officer?

Some schools do care about wildlife and environmental training. A few teachers and educators have learned that an environmental consciousness can be passed on to the young, if we adults know a little about wilderness and wildlife ourselves.

A respect for wild things and wild places is taught successfully when teachers inject environmental thinking into the child's entire curriculum. As a wildlife officer, I have visited and spoken with many school children in their classrooms. They bubble with enthusiasm about wild animals and wild places. It appears to me the young are our answer to future healthy wildlife populations in this country. Children too should know about wildlife officers.

There are only a little over 7,000 state wildlife officers in the nation. There are less than 200 special agents of the U.S. Fish and Wildlife

Service. That might explain why so little is known about wildlife officers. This book would not be complete without my making an attempt to tell you a little more about wildlife officers and what makes them tick.

It takes a special kind of person to be a wildlife officer. The state officers and federal agents I have known and worked with—whether in Wisconsin, Arkansas, Colorado, Maine, New York, Pennsylvania, or Saskatchewan—all possess certain human traits I have not always found in other persons. Let me try to explain what I mean.

I have found that most wildlife officers *live* their job. This is because they believe so deeply in what they are doing. Almost without exception, the officers whom I have known have had a fierce determination to enforce the wildlife and resource regulations—at almost any cost.

Personal discomfort and risk, family inconvenience, lack of financial gain, long and grueling hours, court disappointments, and some-

New Hampshire Conservation Officer Warren Jenkins and U.S. Fish and Wildlife Service Special Agent (Swendsen) cooperate in training session in early 1970s. Agents nowadays are not as likely to wear uniforms. They do, however, have raid jackets and caps for encounters at borders, on special arrests, and on nighttime patrol. *Photo by New Hampshire Fish and Game Department*

times a lack of support from higher management levels all fail to deter the dedicated officer. Very few wildlife officers leave their profession for something more lucrative or less demanding. Most wildlife officers work at being a professional law-enforcement officer for their whole life. Some have given their lives to the protection of the wilderness they believe in.

Who are these state wildlife officers who are devoting their lives to protect our nation's wildlife and wilderness? According to a 1984 survey conducted by the Wildlife Management Institute, there are approximately 7,180 state wildlife officers in the United States. Each state commissions a certain number of officers and empowers them to enforce its natural resource regulations.

Take a look at the following chart, which gives a brief rundown on the approximate number of officers in each state and their titles:

State	Officer Title	Number in State
Alabama	Conservation Officer	145
Alaska	Protection Officer	104
Arizona	Wildlife Manager (includes Special Investigator)	78
Arkansas	Wildlife Officer	135
California	Fish and Game Warden	333
Colorado	District Wildlife Manager	136
Connecticut	Conservation Officer	51
Delaware	Conservation Officer	24
Florida	Wildlife Officer	288
Georgia	Wildlife Ranger	236
Hawaii	Conservation Officer	62
Idaho	Conservation Officer	83
Illinois	Conservation Inspector	124
Indiana	Conservation Officer	189
Iowa	Conservation Officer	81
Kansas	Game Protector	70
Kentucky	Conservation Officer	122
Louisiana	Wildlife Agent	241
Maine	Game Warden	113
Maryland	Wildlife Officer	216
Massachusetts	Natural Resource Officer	67
Michigan	Conservation Officer	219
Minnesota	Conservation Officer	177
Mississippi	Warden	194

State	Officer Title	Number in State
Missouri	Conservation Agent	145
Montana	Warden	80
Nebraska	Conservation Warden	58
Nevada	Fish & Game Agent	27
New Hampshire	Conservation Warden	41
New Jersey	Conservation Warden	50
New Mexico	Conservation Warden	50
New York	Conservation Warden	280
North Carolina	Wildlife Protector	207
North Dakota	Warden	29
Ohio	Game Protector	183
Oklahoma	Game Ranger	106
Oregon	State Police	120
Pennsylvania	Fish and Game Protector (Fish, 86; Game, 150)	236
Rhode Island	Conservation Officer	30
South Carolina	Conservation Officer	200
South Dakota	Conservation Officer	72
Tennessee	Wildlife Officer	158
Texas	Game Management Officer	428
Utah	Conservation Officer	64
Vermont	Game Warden	48
Virginia	Game Warden	120
Washington	Wildlife Agent (Fish, 49; Game, 90)	139
West Virginia	Conservation Officer	109
Wisconsin	Conservation Warden	172
Wyoming	Deputy Game Warden	45

According to the Wildlife Management Institute's wildlife officer surveys, which are taken every four years, there were 12 female officers in the nation in 1976. In 1980 there were 57. There were 106 in 1984. Black officers increased in numbers in the nation from 31 in 1976 to 71 in 1984. Other minority hiring has increased Spanish Americans from 29 to 93, Indians from 40 to 54, and Orientals from 6 to 30.

According to the institute's 1984 survey, there are 45 states in which sidearms are required to be worn as part of the wildlife officer's uniform. Six states make carrying a sidearm optional; a number of these unofficially discourage their officers from carrying sidearms. Most states and the U.S. Fish and Wildlife Service require that their officers and agents take intensive firearms training before they qualify to carry a sidearm. Periodic requalification is also mandatory.

Most state officers are furnished with vehicles. Two-way radios are standard pieces of equipment in almost all officer patrol cars. The 1980 survey indicated that there were 150 state-owned aircraft being used for fish and wildlife law enforcement. In 36 states, officers flew a total of almost 24,000 hours on enforcement details in 1979. The 1984 survey indicated that 157 state-owned and 7 leased aircraft were used for 25,328 hours.

The 1980 and 1984 surveys also indicate substantial changes in state wildlife enforcement in the past four years. The number of officers across the nation has grown by 150—a modest increase. There also appears to be an increased nationwide effort in broad recreational policing. Wildlife officers now have many duties, not all having much to do with fish and wildlife. Officers now enforce littering laws and police state parks in some states; they even enforce laws on pollution and boating and a vast number of other recreational and outdoor regulations.

The survey reports an increasing interest and expenditure by the states in research to determine methods for improving wildlife law enforcement. State legislatures continue to give wildlife enforcement officers more non-wildlife laws to enforce; thus, increased efficiency is mandatory if fish and wildlife are to receive proper protection. Since new authorities and requirements are seldom accompanied by new money, traditional wildlife tasks formerly assigned to the officers are often abandoned.

Training of state wildlife officers is generally becoming more intense and more complicated each year. Wildlife officers continue to become more professional as the techniques of training improve. The U.S. Fish and Wildlife Service carries on a perpetual training program for its agents. It also conducts special training programs for state officers, state enforcement chiefs and supervisors at the nation's Federal Law Enforcement Training Center in Glynco, Georgia.

Unfortunately, I still do not see full cooperation, on both the state and federal levels, between the biological and enforcement branches of wildlife management. Narrow-mindedness and petty jealousies sometimes get in the way. I believe that both sides can work together, as professionals, for the benefit of our wildlife and the public we were hired to serve. If we can not, mediocre management of the resource will be the result.

What does he do? Is he a magician?

Now that we have talked about officer titles and numbers, and a little about who they are, let's talk about what they do and what it takes to become a wildlife officer.

"If you can't swim, you better learn to walk on water." My friends in the Royal Canadian Mounted Police used to hear those words often when they were recruits at their academy in Regina.

A wildlife officer can't be an ordinary person either. He or she must be an expert, or the next thing to it, doing almost everything in the outdoors. Most of all, a wildlife officer must learn quickly about the outdoors and about those people he must deal with in the outdoors. He must be an investigator, interrogator, report writer (like it or not), witness, and sometimes prosecutor.

He must have more than average knowledge about the law, both wildlife laws and laws of criminal procedure. (He may find himself working with prosecutors who are not familiar with wildlife or resource regulations and laws.) He must follow the strict rules of evidence and search and seizure that apply to any policeman, detective, or FBI agent.

He must know about fish and fishing and about big- and small-game hunting techniques and methods. He must develop skills in tracking and trapping, reading maps, camping out, and survival. He must learn how to operate all kinds of boats, vehicles, and specialized pieces of equipment.

He has to be a photographer and mechanic, and he must learn about all types of firearms. Almost all wildlife officers must qualify frequently with a sidearm. It only makes sense for an officer, who contacts in the field more armed persons than any other enforcement officer, to be armed and trained in the use of firearms.

He must also know *when* to draw a firearm. Throughout my career, I stuck by this rule: A wildlife officer should never point a gun at another man unless he is prepared, because of the circumstances, to shoot that man. Bluffing with a firearm can get someone killed—accidentally.

Wildlife officers are often teachers, public speakers, license salesmen, and handlers of nuisance or damage-causing animals. They must answer irate phone calls, arrest violators, counsel juveniles, estimate crop damage, rescue injured wildlife, observe violations accurately, and interview witnesses. When operating in an undercover capacity, they are actors, persuaders, and often diplomats. When outlaws discovered that one of our undercover agents had a pistol hidden in his boot, the agent said, "Sure, I'm armed. How do I know you guys aren't federal agents trying to put me in jail?"

Some officers must perform special duties. Some are pilots and most must be observers from aircraft. Some are accomplished scuba divers, some expert horsemen. Wildlife officers often rescue lost persons in dangerous mountain passes, in deserts, and deep within forests. They also find drowned victims in lakes and rivers.

Many wildlife officers are also classified as peace officers. With this added authority and responsibility, they are often required to act as bodyguards, traffic regulators, riot controllers, and sometimes as firemen or even policemen recruited to help apprehend or arrest wanted criminals in the outdoors.

These are only a few of the skills a wildlife officer is expected to possess. But let me try briefly to give you a few examples of the duties I have been called on to perform, during my thirty-year wildlife-officer career. During previous chapters, you've read about the many kinds of fish and game violations with which wildlife officers become involved. There are many other tasks and duties you might not be aware of.

I've had to act as a policeman apprehending vandals; investigator of thefts of boats, motors, trucks, guns, cows, and timber; fireman; tracker of depredating coyotes and bears; environmental teacher of young and old; even a prosecutor or sometime witness in justice of the peace courts in much of the Midwest, Northeast, and in some southern states. I was once called upon to testify in the Queen's Court in Saskatchewan.

I have had the unpleasant task of dragging the bottoms of many Wisconsin lakes and rivers for drowning victims, never "enjoying" the success of recovering as many as six bodies in one month. I have climbed down from the top of New Hampshire's Mt. Washington, where winter winds have been recorded at 263 miles per hour, to a hidden lake where I planted trout in 42-degree waters. I told you about the eaglet I helped carry to the top of the 80-foot Wisconsin pine, to put it into the 700-pound nest of a pair of bald eagles.

I have flown waterfowl surveys up and down the Mississippi and Wisconsin Rivers, the flooding Red River of the North, the northeast and coastal states, and across many of the Canadian provinces, from Alberta to New Brunswick.

I have launched and landed boats, and motored lakes, rivers, ponds, flowages, and the Atlantic Ocean to check hunters and fishermen in over half the states of the nation, and many areas along the Mexican and Canadian borders.

I have investigated those suspected of murder, theft, arson, illegal entry, deer shining, fish spearing and seining, fishing or hunting without

This photo of Swendsen was snapped by his trip partner Howard Lovrien when they stopped for a lunch break on a Mississippi River sandbar near LaCrosse, Wisconsin. They were checking the conditions of the water and the waterfowl from Minneapolis south to Clinton, Iowa, a project that involved several days of running the locks. Information gathered on trips like this helped them plan their fall work in waterfowl protection. *Photo by Howard Lovrien, U.S. Fish and Wildlife Service*

licenses or with fraudulent licenses, taking overbags or out-of-season game and fish, trapping illegally, and dealing illegally in millions of dollars' worth of wildlife fur.

I arrested a deer hunter so intoxicated that when I had him in my car on his way to jail, he said suddenly, "There's a deer." He tried to get at his confiscated rifle in the back seat to shoot a big buck that was standing alongside the road.

"We better get out of here." The voice I heard was close to panic. I was driving a forest protection truck into the middle of a raging forest fire with only a sixteen-year-old boy manning the hoses to try to stop the howling fire from crossing our road before it roared into a group of lakeside cottages. I will never forget the sound of the oncoming crowning fire, almost drowning out the young boy's voice, as it suddenly picked up speed in the thirty-mile-per-hour summer winds and forced us to retreat. It soon burned its way through twenty cottages and thirty sections of prime Wisconsin timber. The boy used our hoses to keep our truck from bursting into flames as we roared away.

Dave Swendsen poses with a sample of equipment that wildlife officers use. The collection is by no means complete. Each officer requires special gear according to jurisdiction, climate, water areas, mountains, or coastlands. How many of the items in this picture can you identify? Gear shown here includes gun case, shotgun, regulation book, plug-in spotlight, atlas, hipboots, handcuffs, snub-nosed revolver, .357 service revolver, credentials, notebook, hunting knife, pocket knife, shotgun-plug checker, fingerprint kit and marking tags, blue stoplight, flashlight, ear protectors, tape recorder, .357 ammunition, camera with flash, thermometers, tripod, 30-power spotting scope, binoculars, cold-weather suit, camouflage hat, cane, raingear, come-along (for getting vehicles unstuck), lunchbag and stainless-steel thermos, jack, survival-gear bag, life preserver, first-aid kit, plastic bucket with various ropes, tool kit for boat and car. *Photo by Thomas A. Greene of Rhode Island*

I've investigated many hunting accidents, including the shooting of a deer hunter by his wife during a deer drive. The wife of the dead man married another member of the deer drive just months after her husband was buried. She married a man she had been seeing prior to the "accidental shooting."

"Put down the gun and let's talk," I said as compassionately as I could. I was talking to a man through a barn wall. We talked for three hours as he threatened to take his own life because his wife had left him. I tried everything I could think of to get him to toss his pearl-handled revolver out to me. I failed. He put the gun in his mouth and pulled the trigger.

I have been shot at, sworn at, and swung at. I have been lied to and hidden from; I've received payoff offers and life-threatening phone calls, and have had deer shiners try to run over me with their car. I've worked nighttime deer shiners from the air as an observer, when we had to use a car's headlights at one end of the runway and another car's taillights at the far end for us to land.

I've apprehended the same person three times in three years for the same offense. He asked, "When are you going to leave me alone?" My answer? "When you decide to stay within the law." I caught another person three nights in a row and am aware of a lawyer who was caught violating migratory bird laws twice in the same day.

I've had to shoot a 500-pound bear devastating backwoods farm-ers' cornfields. I've been outwitted by a big (almost 50-pound) coyote that methodically killed 65 sheep, one at a time for 65 nights. The state trapper and I tried vainly to catch her in a trap. She was too wise; she turned the traps over and, with her pups, continued to kill sheep until the few remaining were moved to a pen near the farmhouse. The big coyote was hunted with dogs and shot the following winter. She weighed 46 pounds, the biggest coyote in my record book.

I have walked within 10 feet of a big buck at night, shining a bright light into his eyes. I've seen spawning walleyed pike so thick in a streambed that you could almost walk on their backs. I found that old muskies are quite habitual; they loll around in the same place at about the same time almost every day. I've weighed in 40-, 50-, and even 56-pound muskies.

"Help, I'm drowning." I heard a voice coming from the river. A 90-pound sturgeon, snagged illegally below the dam, rolled back out into the rushing water and pulled the violator into the swirling water. Had I not been there, he might have drowned.

I have seen 4-pound bluegills, caught 4-pound flounder, and have landed 5- and 10-pound steelhead trout. These were trout that had come up out of Lake Superior to spawn in streams so small that there was hardly enough water for the big fish to swim. I've seen wood ticks so thick on a summertime bear that when he was shot dead trying to break through a family's window screen for some food, the bear still looked alive because of the moving ticks.

I've chased fish and game violators through the woods, up rivers, across lakes, and down back roads in my patrol car at seventy miles per hour, and on highways at such speeds that my two-way radio antennae shorted out on the car fender.

I've been run off the road by drunken drivers and have had my tires slashed. I've had hunters drive away and leave me stuck in the mud, ten miles from nowhere. But I've also had people go far out of their way to drive me to my car, even though my appearance at their hunting grounds meant a later trip to court.

I've had to arrest neighbors, boy scout leaders, ministers, priests, old women, juveniles, mental patients, policemen, detectives, mayors, city clerks, bankers, firemen, businessmen, lawyers, doctors, and foreigners who couldn't speak English. I've also been involved in the apprehension of a few senators and a governor or two—all for fish and game law violations.

I've helped convict fish and game law violators using plaster casts of tire and foot prints, fingerprints off beer bottles and guns, photographs taken through a telescope, bird and animal temperatures to prove time of death, and blood and hair samples linking the wildlife outlaw to the time and place of the violation.

I have dug into garbage and litter piles to extract addresses and names linking people to evidence. I have used shell casings, rifle serial numbers, and extractor marks to prove the ownership of unclaimed firearms found at the scene.

I have also used handwriting samples, mine detectors, night vision scopes, confessions, witness statements, and retrieving dogs to convict wildlife outlaws of their crimes against the wilderness.

I have worked on fish and game and other outdoor violators at all hours of the day or night. I've apprehended violators when I was cold, hungry, sick, tired, lost, frightened, nervous, wet, hot, threatened, intimidated, and outnumbered. I once had to hitchhike a ride on the highway to catch up with some hunters; I had watched them from a mile away, violating the goose regulations.

"I'm a conservation officer [or federal agent]. You are under arrest." I have said these words, arrested people, and made searches in barns, taverns, warehouses, kitchens, factories, stores, cornfields, and in cars and boats of every description. I have also had to make arrests in railroad cars, trucks, all-night restaurants, sleazy bars, pool halls, shopping malls, and on mountains, in caves, airplanes, private hunting lodges, private offices, and locker plants.

I've watched people who were caught in the act of violating fish and game regulations, lie, become angry and violent and even say, "The boy did it." I've seen them run, drive like madmen, hide in outhouses, fight, get sick, cry, threaten, pull rank, panic, attempt bribes, faint, have heart attacks and bowel movements, throw expensive guns into a pile of rocks or deep water, or leave the guns behind and never return to claim them.

I have also seen violators of the fish and game laws be truthful, upright, courageous, honest, humble, regretful, and helpful. Many people show strength of character under very embarrassing and stressful circumstances.

But in all, I have not seen it all. I have not been everywhere with everyone, through everything. No wildlife officer, no person, has. Each time I have contacted another person in the outdoors, when he is using

Among Swendsen's duties as a Special Agent in Charge were television appearances such as this one on an agricultural show of Boston's Channel 5. Here his aim was to inform the public about the duties of a federal wildlife agent and to show and discuss some of an agent's equipment.

or abusing the wilderness or its wildlife, something new happens. No two people react the same way to "Good morning, I'm a conservation warden [or special agent with the Fish and Wildlife Service]. I'd like to see your license."

Wildlife officers would have to know all about the wilderness and its wildlife and all there is to know about people to have all the answers. No officer, no person, ever will. Maybe that's what makes life so interesting and worth living. Maybe that's why wildlife officers, state and federal, think that their life and their profession are so special.

Oh yes, at times we have to be magicians.

Becoming a wildlife officer

Because so many young people have asked me through the years about becoming a wildlife officer, I think this book would be incomplete if I didn't tell briefly how I ended up wearing a badge for most of my life.

Many young men and women think they would like to become wildlife officers. They have dreams of hunting, fishing, and having their very own cabin in the woods. The awful truth is that wardens seldom have time to fish, they rarely have a chance to get away from hunters to go hunting themselves, and few can afford to have their own cabins in the woods.

A wildlife officer's job becomes more than a full-time profession. There are never enough hours in the day. And to be effective, an officer must be out when the outdoor people are out. It is not a nine-to-five job.

I had never planned on being a wildlife officer. I guess I had heard there was such a creature, and I had seen the usual pictures of a man with a badge stepping out from behind a tree to confront a young child at a "no fishing" hole. But like most people, I had yet to see a game warden in the woods, and I was twenty-five years old.

I did think I wanted to work outdoors in the wilderness, especially in the forests. The nearby college of my choice (the price was right, $60 per semester) didn't offer a forestry degree then, so I majored in courses that turned out to be tailor-made for someone who, unknowingly, would be enforcing the state fish and game laws. I took such courses as biology, plant ecology, zoology, botany, dendrology (study of trees), wildlife management, and courses in agronomy, meteorology, bacteriology, animal husbandry, soils, and the properties of wood.

After flunking chemistry because I played on too many basketball teams (and had some strange idea that university professors graded on a curve—"everyone couldn't flunk chemistry"), I turned to courses in geology, water resources, and engineering. I also got some credits in journalism which, aside from my four-fingered typing, I really enjoyed. I couldn't ignore that I still had to retake chemistry to graduate. I finally did (and it was still tough). A course in law and several in wildlife law enforcement would have been extremely helpful, but few colleges offered such courses then; not many offer wildlife enforcement in their curriculum today. Through the years, in on-the-job training situations, I have been fortunate to learn and later teach wildlife law-enforcement techniques in many parts of the country.

After discharge from the Air Force, I was working on my master's degree in journalism, had just married, and was ready to get out and make some big money.

"Why don't you take the state warden exam?" A friend did talk me into taking the exam. I guess I didn't look at the fine print pay scale. I placed thirteenth, a number—good or bad—that continues to follow me wherever I go. Thirteenth seemed pretty low to me and I didn't expect to hear from the state again. But I soon found myself being interviewed for a warden's job.

Before I knew it, I was signing papers that committed me to put on the badge of a Wisconsin conservation warden. I learned I would be heading into the north country, where there were supposed to be more wild animals than people, and a lot of wild people too. I was scheduled to receive my badge and gun on June 13, 1955, and I began my warden career with a starting salary of $3800 per year.

After five expensive years of college (working as I went) and several years of low-pay Air Force time, with my new wife and our joint savings account of $37.13, the number 13 already seemed to be indicating our financial future. But like many young newlyweds, I thought, who needs money when you're in love with your woman and your work?

All of a sudden I found myself selected, commissioned, given badge and gun, and sent on the road north (alone) to enforce the state wildlife laws. Jackie was left behind temporarily to continue working at the state capital, like it or not.

A picture poster I saw years ago on a sheriff's wall reminds me now of my sudden officer status. It was a drawing of a cross-eyed, dim-witted man. Under the man's picture was this statement: "Yesterday I don't know what a *saleman* were, today I *are* one." Maybe that's how I was beginning to feel in my new role as a just-hired conservation warden.

I had fished trout, hunted a few pheasants, and had been an Eagle Scout. Other than that, I had little experience in the ways of wildlife. I had never seen a live deer in the woods, had never been in a courtroom, and had only read the word *arrest* in the newspapers.

I did have a piece of paper from the University of Wisconsin that had B.S. printed on it. But I began to wonder just what the B.S. really stood for. Stumbling into the north country, I soon found out that I wasn't going to B.S. any of those backwoods natives with a piece of paper from some big-town college.

I learned as time went on that northwoods outlaws can only be impressed with a piece of paper that has the words ARREST or SEARCH WARRANT printed across the top and the judge's signature at the bottom. (And sometimes even that doesn't impress them.)

It wasn't easy becoming a game warden in those days. It's not easy today. In my day, college degrees were not usually required. According to the Wildlife Management Institute's 1984 survey, sixteen states now require a B.S. degree of those wanting to become officers; seven states require at least two years of college. And except for Louisiana and Wisconsin, which have no educational requirement, all the rest require a high school diploma. Special agents of the F&W Service must have a college degree plus years of wildlife law enforcement experience, or a background and education that compensate.

Special agent candidates must compete with thousands of applicants who apply each time ten or twenty vacancies are announced. There are less than 200 special agents in the nation today. They are usually selected from the ranks of other federal law-enforcement agencies or from the most qualified and most experienced state wildlife-officer candidates who apply.

Today's starting salaries for wildlife officers are quite different from my early days twenty or so years ago. Salary ranges vary greatly from state to state; starting salaries for state officers can range from less than $10,000 to more than $20,000 per year. Applicants must contact state fish and game agencies for current figures.

Special agents of the U.S. Fish and Wildlife Service, once attaining GS-11 journeyman status, receive approximately $28,000 a year depending somewhat on their years of service. They also receive premium pay for working long overtime and irregular, unscheduled overtime hours.

States occasionally open their hiring doors to new officers. Each state will give examinations, physicals, and interviews prior to hiring. The federal register for special agents opens ordinarily every few years, but only a few carefully selected agents are put on. Hiring in both state and federal wildlife officer positions has been very restricted in the past few years because of budget shortages at both levels of government. Interested candidates must check directly with those agencies involved. State officer candidates should contact the personnel departments of the state fish and wildlife agency in which they are interested. Special agent candidates should contact the law enforcement division of the U.S. Fish and Wildlife Service in Washington, D.C., for information about future agent openings.

"How can I become a wildlife officer?" I've been asked this question many, many times. Through the years I have also received written inquiries from young people interested in becoming state or federal officers. Some of these conscientious people write or call to say they have taken a correspondence course on conservation subjects. They tell me, "I have now completed the course and am eager and ready to go to work as a wildlife officer, state or federal." I have to tell them that these courses cover the basics of conservation, but they are not sufficient preparation for the career of a wildlife officer. Much more schooling and experience are required, and I advise young people to contact the proper state or federal agency for more information while they are still in high school.

I remember just how I felt about my new job during my first months as a state officer in Wisconsin. (I can remember almost as if it were yesterday.) I had just checked out some fishermen at a quiet landing on the Chippewa River. The fishermen were nice people and everything seemed in order. We talked about the river and muskies as we sipped a cup of coffee together. As I shoved their boat back into the current and waved, I couldn't help but say to myself, these men are professionals making a lot of money and I'm sure well able to afford a fishing trip on the Chippewa. But I wouldn't trade my long hours and low pay with any of them. I knew I had the best darn job in the world. I had a feeling of doing something creative for the wildlife and those people who need wilderness in their lives. I still feel much the same today as I did then. It can be the best darn job in the world.

It can be dangerous

"Please hand me your gun." That statement can cause some hunters to react irrationally, sometimes violently.

Being a wildlife officer can be dangerous. What other law-enforcement officer contacts more people carrying firearms than a wildlife officer? Most of these contacts do not result in any violent conduct, but none of these gun-involved hunter checks can actually be called routine.

When a wildlife officer starts to treat any of these contacts carelessly or routinely, he opens himself up to a certain amount of danger. Some hunters react strangely or overly possessive when you ask them to hand over their firearms during a license check in the field. It takes a lot of tact and smoothness, on the part of the wildlife officer, to eliminate violence during some of these so-called "routine" hunter checks. Nighttime checks are even more hazardous, as darkness seems to cause humans to act differently than they do in broad daylight.

The Wildlife Management Institute's 1980 survey indicated that approximately 116 wildlife officers had been killed in the performance of their duties. Many more have been seriously injured or narrowly escaped serious injury while protecting the resources. The 1984 survey shows the four-year assault rate on wildlife officers was 2.72 per 100 officers. At that rate almost 82 percent of the wildlife officers would be assaulted during a thirty-year career. Nearly all assaults are by people armed with guns and/or knives. Even though he becomes very good at sizing up the person he is checking, an officer can never be sure that that person will not turn violent. This makes him very vulnerable. But if he were to approach every hunter suspiciously, as if he expected violence, the officer would soon be looking for a new job. His best safety precaution is not to become careless. He must also continue to train himself so that his reactions to violence are automatic.

Let me describe for you some of the dangerous situations I have been close to—times when the job, like life, was not all roses.

Coward by the side of the road

Late one fall evening, Minnesota conservation warden Jim Akley was driving his patrol car along a back road near the Mille Lac Lake Indian reservation when a shotgun blast tore the windshield off his vehicle, sending glass into his face. Remarkably, Jim, an Indian himself, was not seriously injured. The person who fired that cowardly shot was never apprehended. There was little doubt, from the investigation that followed, that whoever pulled the trigger had only one intention: to kill warden Jim Akley.

Jim was a hard worker. He treated everyone the same. He was respected by those he dealt with. His hard work and determination to enforce the fish and game laws in a wild country was too much for some coward who hid in the trees and tried to end Jim's life.

Jim later transferred to Orr, Minnesota, where he continued to perform his warden duties as a professional officer and professional person. I am sad to report that Jim died of a heart attack several years later. The wilderness, along with his young family, misses Jim Akley.

Carrying lead

In March of 1962, Vic Blazevic, special agent of the U.S. F&W Service, was shot twice with shotgun blasts to his face, neck, hand, and body, while attempting to arrest two out-of-season duck hunters. The illegal hunters tried to escape from Vic and a rookie Illinois officer by creeping across a cornfield at the edge of an old oxbow off the Mississippi River.

Suddenly Vic heard a shot and felt pain in his left hand. He pulled out his service revolver and turned in the direction of the first blast when his assailant fired again. Blazevic was looking almost directly down the gun barrel on the second blast.

"I saw the flame come out like a blow-torch," Vic told me years later when we were working together on the marshes of the Midwest. He told me he went down with the second shot; blood was pouring from his face and neck. Barely able to see, he knew he would have to get out of there or bleed to death. Fortunately, the assailant had used his last two shells on Vic.

Quick hospitalization and knowledgeable doctors saved Vic's eye, which had been struck in the socket and retina. His head looked like a pumpkin the next day. He still carries shot in his head, neck, and body.

Vic was the senior resident agent in Chicago when I was ASAC in Minneapolis. He went on to become the special agent in charge of investigations in Washington, D.C., before he retired several years ago. The man convicted of assaulting agent Blazevic served a term in prison. He is now paroled and back in the community.

A 30-30 in the eye

Conservation warden Jim Goberville apprehended a man spearing

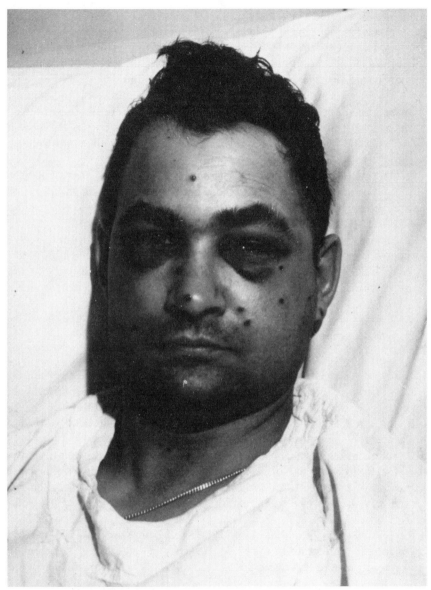

In mid-March one year, Special Agent Victor A. Blazevic was chasing some illegal hunters at dusk in an Illinois cornfield. One hunter pointed a shotgun at him and fired twice. After a harrowing trip and profuse bleeding, Blazevic reached a hospital. Recalling the experience and looking at his photo, Blazevic says, "I looked considerably worse the day before. My head was swelled up, and I looked like a pumpkin. When I looked in the mirror the day after it happened, I didn't recognize myself." The shooter was sentenced to federal prison. *Photo by F. Charles Kniffin, U.S. Fish and Wildlife Service*

fish late one night on a Rice Lake, Wisconsin, stream. The violator was placed under arrest after a wet tussle on the stream. The soaked outlaw asked Goberville if he would take him home so he could change his clothes and explain to his wife that he was on his way to jail. The violator said his wife would be worried about him.

Goberville, a thoughtful and understanding man, took the spearer home. The spearer invited the veteran warden into the house and told him to sit at the kitchen table; he gave Goberville a cup of coffee and went into the bedroom. He said he would quickly change and then go willingly to jail.

The next thing warden Goberville saw was the business end of a 30-30 rifle; it was like looking into a cannon. The armed violator told Goberville, "Get the hell out of my house or I will blow your damn head off." The warden thoughtfully complied.

Goberville returned shortly with the sheriff and several state police officers. They ordered the outlaw out of the house, placed him under arrest, cuffed him, and hauled him (clean clothes and all) off to the county jail. He now faced charges more serious than spearing fish.

Mr. Conservation

Bob Markle was a conservation warden who cared a great deal about his work. He cared even more about young people and wildlife. He was liked by everyone but the hardened fish and game outlaws, and they respected him. Bob was Mr. Conservation to the young and old alike in Ashland County, Wisconsin, where he had been stationed as a warden for many years.

One dark night, Bob chased some fish spearers down a narrow, twisting road in his patrol car. He had chased violators down this same road many times before. On a bad turn in the road, Bob rolled his patrol car off into the trees. He died that night, a victim of his dedication.

The people of Ashland County missed Bob Markle. They wanted everyone to remember how he had died. If you drive south from Mellen today, you will be travelling down the Bob Markle Memorial Highway.

Live decoy

Don Blais was a federal agent who loved his job. He loved people, especially his lovely wife and four sparkling children. Don was originally from Rhode Island and was brought up on seafood. He had a real knowledge of the outdoors, especially the New England coastal environment. Don had first been a Rhode Island state officer and then a special agent for the U.S. Fish and Wildlife Service in New Hampshire and then Connecticut.

I succeeded Don in New Hampshire. He left only good feelings there. Fellow officers and the public liked Don Blais, because of his absolute honesty and never-ending enthusiasm for protecting the wildlife he loved so much. Don had apprehended waterfowl violators up and down the East coast. He will be remembered best by fellow officers for his punt gun arrest on the Maine–New Hampshire line in a snowstorm in the 1960s.

A punt gun is a cannon-like weapon, filled with nuts and bolts and projectiles of all description. It is charged with a huge load of black powder and set out on the edge of the water where ducks and geese normally congregate to rest. The gun is set off into the flock, sending out its death-dealing projectiles in a massive explosion. Don's punt gun case was the last one made on the East coast that I am aware of. The gun is on display at the Fish and Game Headquarters in Augusta, Maine.

Don was on assignment in Delaware during the opening of the waterfowl hunting season. He and several other state and federal officers were checking hunters early one morning. Don discovered a live decoy on one of the hunting ponds used by a gun club. (A live decoy is a duck—or in this case a goose—with clipped wings, staked or kept in the immediate vicinity of the hunting blinds to attract and call in vulnerable wild birds for easy and illegal shooting.) Don and the other officers knew that to prosecute the illegal hunters, someone would have to capture the live goose and hold it for evidence.

"I'll get it," Don told fellow officers. Always a volunteer, Don slogged out into the cold, deep water and black mud with a landing net to capture the bird. The other officers suddenly saw him go down as if he had been struck from behind. Don's heart had stopped. Other officers got to him, but could not revive him. His life ended on one of his beloved ponds, doing what he believed in most.

When his life stopped, with it went a man known to all for his loving concern and dedication to our wildlife. Don's family, along with hundreds of uniformed wildlife officers, conducted a special funeral service for this wildlife officer who wanted no frills, even in death. He requested, before he died, that he be buried in a pine box. As I watched the pine box being lowered into its final resting place, I knew the outdoors would be just a little better place because of Don Blais. I know it's not the same without him.

Gun tussle

Some hunters do not want to give up their guns to a wildlife officer, even when it is just for a routine check for a waterfowl plug (to limit the number of shells) or to see if the gun is loaded when carried in an automobile. Just handing a gun to a warden seems to upset some hunters. One of my most reliable deputies all year around was a forest ranger named Major Miller. I used to kid Major about how his name would sound if he were a captain in the Army, Captain Major Miller.

Late one afternoon during the Wisconsin deer season, Major's fellow ranger, Jerry Jackeline, called me on the radio to request that I come as soon as possible.

"We're having a tussle over a firearm up here and need some help."

I couldn't get all the details of what was going on, but heard enough to know that I should get there as soon as possible. As I rammed my patrol vehicle into gear and headed north with my red light flashing, I received a second radio message from Jerry.

"Major has hold of one end of a rifle and your old friend Oscar Bramley has hold of the other end. Neither will let go." I hoped that Major had hold of the right end.

Ten minutes later I skidded to a stop beside the two men. Both were holding fast and hard to Bramley's deer rifle. The gun now rested on the hood of the hunter's car. The other hunters (three of them) and the second ranger stood off to the side of the vehicle and watched the struggle. I bounced out of my vehicle on the run. "Oscar, let go of that gun *now*," I said, "or I'll have you in jail in thirty minutes."

By the time I reached the two struggling men and put my left hand on the gun barrel, Oscar was releasing his grip. The gun was not pointed at anyone at the moment.

With my right hand I reached into my back pocket for my blackjack. My intention was to come down with the blackjack on Oscar's wrist. But he let go, just as I pulled the persuader from my pocket. Major let go too. I stepped back, swung the gun away from everyone, and jacked five live rounds out onto the ground. I told Oscar to get into my car.

I told the other hunters to "stay where you are." The second ranger would see to that. Major and I stepped off to the side; he filled me in on the drama that had taken place before my arrival.

About an hour before, as the two rangers turned into the old tote road ahead of us, they met Oscar's car coming out. Looking down into the car from the cab of the big forestry truck, the rangers saw all the hunters in the car start to shuffle around with their firearms. It appeared they were trying to get the guns unloaded.

Carrying a loaded or uncased firearm in a motor vehicle was, and is now, a violation of Wisconsin law. Carrying a loaded firearm in a moving vehicle is a dangerous practice that has cost the life of many an unbelieving hunter, or even a passenger.

Major explained how he and Jerry had bailed out of the truck to apprehend the hunters before they succeeded in unloading and casing their rifles to avoid arrest. When the rangers got to the car, all the hunters, except the driver and front-seat passenger, had succeeded in their endeavors.

The passenger gave up his firearm to one ranger; but when Major reached for Oscar Bramley's rifle, the tussle began. Major kept telling Oscar he was under arrest and he should let go of the gun.

"You're not taking my gun, you ###**&¢! warden," Oscar kept saying. The two men, according to Major, tugged and struggled with the rifle, causing the barrel to point in dangerous directions. Everyone else scattered to get out of the way. Eventually, the battle over the gun ended in a stalemate on the hood of the car. That's when I arrived.

I got into the car with Oscar. I told him we were going straight to the judge. His hunting companions could pick him up in town if the judge didn't put him in jail. Before we left for town, I told Oscar and the other hunters we could handle fish and game violations like gentlemen, but fighting with enforcement officers at the scene is another matter.

The judge did not put Oscar in jail. He fined him and put him on probation for one year. This was Oscar's second offense in two years. Oscar didn't want to go to jail. I knew that. I had arrested him last year for shining deer. He knew what it was like to hear the cell door clank shut.

A sharp knife

It was a very dark night. My game-manager partner, Don Balser, and I were getting sleepy. It was about 1:30 A.M. We hadn't seen a car for two hours. We said we would give it another half hour, then head for home. I had received information that deer shiners were making good use of the field we could see about one-half mile away.

I was just reaching for my ignition switch when we saw lights. A pickup truck suddenly appeared from a nearby driveway and started down our road. The truck drove into the field, drove to the back and a light darted out across the field. When the pickup truck came out of the field, we blocked the car with our red light flashing.

My deputy jumped out of the vehicle and headed for the driver's side of the pickup truck; I headed for the passenger side. We saw the driver jump from the truck and head off into the woods on the dead run. I saw something glisten in the moonlight as Don took off after him, calling out, "Conservation wardens, you're under arrest."

I hit the passenger side of the truck just as a second man burst out almost into my arms. I grabbed the burly, rough-looking man and said loudly, "Conservation warden, you're under arrest." I hauled the man around to the front end of the truck, spun him around, and did a quick frisk. I pulled out a razor-sharp hunting knife from a sheath he carried on his belt. I didn't know what to do with the knife, so I slipped it carefully into my jacket pocket. I could see a teenaged boy still sitting in the cab of the truck. He appeared to be too stunned to move. I shouted at him to stay where he was. He didn't move.

The man I had now arrested started to balk when I told him to put his hands behind his back so I could cuff him. I could see a box of .22-caliber shells and what appeared to be a hunting license protruding from his shirt pocket.

"Hand me the license and shells."

"You want dem, you take dem from me."

This was new business to me. This was my first year as a warden.

"Resisting arrest will only make things worse for you."

The man's answer was to raise his hands in a defensive posture and repeat, "You want dem, you take dem from me."

I took a quick look at the teenager in the truck and then lunged at the man. We hit the ground together; he was swinging at me with his fist. I reached around behind his head and pulled his neck farther back then was his normal morning exercise. I had been lucky. He was strong as a bull and raging mad. I pulled his head back another inch and said, "Had enough?" He grunted and relaxed.

In one minute I rolled him over and put my knee in his back. I pulled my cuffs from my belt and jammed them onto his wrists. I hoisted him to his feet, pushed him to the back of my car, and snapped the cuffs into a big ring I had bolted to my bumper just for that purpose—a trick Big Ed had taught me.

No sooner did I get outlaw number one hooked to the bumper, sitting on the ground, when back came the driver escorted by my partner. The big man was swearing and arguing about being hassled on his own property, while just looking for a "lost cow."

"Where's the gun you took from the truck?" I asked the new arrival. "You don't need a gun to look for a cow."

"I don't know nothing about no gun. Get off my property before I throw you off."

"Stay right there," I said, looking at my equally inexperienced partner for support. I wanted him to watch Cow-finder while I went to the truck to look for the gun. The boy still sat unmoving. I saw .22-caliber shells all over the floor of the cab. I flashed my bright light around the outside of the truck.

Under the running board in the grass between the front and back wheels, I saw the gun. It lay quite dry in the dew-covered grass. I picked up the Mosberg .22 rifle and found that the magazine had been pulled out. But in doing so, Cow-finder had scattered shells on the floor of the truck. Several shells had hung up in the magazine. One shell still remained in the firing chamber. I must have seen Cow-finder pull out the magazine in the moonlight when he ran off into the woods. He had thrown it somewhere out there hoping we wouldn't find it.

"OK Don, I've got the gun." I went up to the second man, only to find him recoiling and taking up a defensive stance just as his hand-cuffed friend had ten moments before.

"You are under arrest," I said. "Now don't give me a hard time like your friend. I've had enough of that for one night."

"You ain't takin' me to no jail."

"Get up against my car and spread your legs." I was losing my patience.

"You want me in jail, then pull that gun you have in your belt and use it. That's the only way you're getting me behind bars."

I was pretty damn inexperienced, but I could still hear Big Ed's words, "You never pull your weapon, except in self-defense; and when you pull it, be prepared to shoot someone."

Don was standing back, wanting to help but not knowing what to do. I thought, Well, Swendsen, he's calling your bluff. Now what?

I must have seen it in the cowboy movies, because no one prepares a young warden for this turn of events: I reached down and unbuckled my gun belt and tossed the gun over to my partner. Then, very dramatically, I pulled out my new leather blackjack and said, "OK, I'll go a round with you too, but you can see I'm not playing any game with you." I raised the blackjack and said to Don, "Get the kid out of the truck and call the sheriff on the radio."

I knew the sheriff was twenty miles away, in bed, and his dispatcher couldn't get us any help for an hour. But I wanted Cow-finder to think we had lots of help coming in from the right flank. I hoped the big man wouldn't notice the newness of my blackjack. It was going to be my first swing with it.

Suddenly, to my surprise, my opponent dropped his hands and stepped back.

"Alright, alright, I'll do what you say. Put that thing away."

As my second conquest moved to the car I said, "*Lean*, hands on the hood. Spread your feet." I kicked his feet apart to make sure he was off balance while I searched him.

"Don, get my other cuffs from the car."

I had an old rusty pair on the seat. Soon we had both men cuffed and in the car with the boy. We finished our investigation of the scene, locked up the truck, and headed for town.

The two men spent the night in jail and later paid a $100 fine for shining while in possession of a firearm. I felt I was lucky no one had gotten hurt.

When I went to take the knife out of my pocket, I found it had sliced its way out. I found it the next day on the ground where our short wrestling match had taken place.

I found out why the two men didn't want to go to jail that night. They had been there before. The first man had stuck someone with his knife in a barroom fight. The second had been convicted of shooting another trapper in the leg for supposedly stealing a muskrat from his traps. Both men knew what jail was all about. Through the years, I found that something happens to a man as he empties his pockets, takes off his belt, and hears the cell door clank shut.

Blood in the woods

My flashlight stabbed into the inky darkness. Fearful, I ran through the heavy woods toward the scuffling sounds ahead. My heart skipped a beat as a revolver shot split the night air, just ahead of me. I ran faster. Several minutes later I came to a small clearing.

Two men were fighting on the ground. They were covered with blood. One of our deputies was standing over the two men trying to pry them apart. He was trying to distinguish, through the blood, which of the battlers was our fellow warden and which was the escaping deer shiner.

As I panted up to the clearing, I recognized a binocular strap around the neck of one of the men. Then they rolled over and I saw the badge flash from my light. I reached down and grabbed the other wrestling man by the back of the neck. With the help of the deputy, I twisted and jerked the bloody man backwards. He was forced to release his arm stranglehold on our warden. We dragged the struggling man off to the side. I turned him over on his stomach. I held his arms behind his back. He still wanted to do battle as I continued to hold him face down.

"You're under arrest."

The deputy quickly went to the aid of our downed warden. Neither man had been shot. Both men were bleeding severely from head and facial cuts. The deputy was able to help warden Kern to his feet. After catching his breath, Kern said he was okay.

We started back toward our cars with the deer shiner. Other wardens waited for our arrival in a field next to the woods, with the second night hunter handcuffed in the back seat of a patrol car. Two dead deer lay in the field next to my car. The lights from another patrol vehicle silhouetted them in the otherwise extreme darkness of the night.

By now, our captive had stopped struggling. I walked him over to my car.

"Step over to the car, turn around, and lean on your hands. I'm going to search you for weapons." Because we had enough help in the woods, I had not cuffed him as I ordinarily would. I was also cautious in handling him since I did not know what injuries he had suffered during the battle in the woods.

Just as my captive turned toward the car, my supervisor, Bill Waggoner, said, "Just a minute, Bert." (Bill had had encounters with my captive before.) "I saw you drop something out of your pocket."

Bill stepped over quickly and picked up three unfired cartridges from the ground where Bert had been standing. Bill handed them to me. Bert didn't say anything.

"They are thirty-two special," Bill said, "the same caliber as the gun we just found hanging by its trigger guard in the bushes over there." He pointed over toward the edge of the woods. Both Bert and his partner denied ownership of the gun then, and later in court.

The gun had a night scope built onto it. It was a specially constructed telescopic sight with custom-made crosshairs. The sight worked best in the nighttime when other sights needed more light. The gun had recently been fired. Its owner wasn't far away.

Later, bullets were taken from the deer. They were proven to have been fired from this weapon. There was dew on everything that night. The gun was dry. It hadn't been hanging in the bushes very long. We still had to tie the gun to Bert and his partner.

After trying to talk Bert into the patrol car, so as not to injure him further, I had to finally put him into the back seat. He hadn't quit fighting yet. I hustled him off to the sheriff's office. I called ahead by radio and had a doctor waiting there to treat both Bert and warden Kern for their wounds.

Bert would not let the doctor treat him until his brother got there.

"I want my brother here to see that the doctor won't do more harm to me than good."

The doctor later testified in court that by refusing immediate treatment, Bert had seriously jeopardized the sight of his eye. He lost that sight from the injury.

Kern's head was badly cut. When Kern was chasing Bert through the woods, Bert had turned on the warden and slammed him to the ground with a blow from his flashlight. Kern later testified in court that he blocked Bert's second swing with his arm. Kern then swung back at Bert with his flashlight, hitting Bert across the side of the head, injuring Bert's eye.

Kern also testified that the shot was fired as Bert grabbed Kern's binocular straps and tried to twist them tight to choke the downed warden. Kern reached inside his shoulder holster for his revolver and attempted to hit Bert over the head with it. Bert grabbed the gun and attempted to turn the business end of it into Kern's stomach. Before he could, the gun went off into the woods. That is when the deputy and I arrived on the scene.

Bert was charged with assault on an officer in the performance of his duty. Bert's partner was charged with shining and shooting two deer. Bert's partner was found not guilty because we couldn't prove the gun belonged to either man at the scene.

Bert's assault trial was held several months later than his partner's deer-shining hearing. By the time of Bert's trial, we were better prepared to prove ownership of the gun. We found a box of 32 special, unfired cartridges on a dresser in Bert's house (via a search warrant). We also traced the serial numbers on the gun to a retailer in the next town. Still no one would come forth to testify that the gun was Bert's. They stated that they feared their houses would be torched if they spoke up.

Just before the trial time, with the help of the Wisconsin crime lab, we came up with another way to tie the gun to Bert. It should not have been necessary to prove that the gun was Bert's because we had charged him with assault. But unless we could tie Bert to the dead deer, a jury would turn him loose on the assault charge. I knew how things were done in my county.

"I never saw that gun before," Bert testified. He got on the stand with a patch over his eye. He denied ownership of the gun. He testified that he had heard shooting in the fields behind his house that night so he and his friend ran out to see what was happening. He said they saw a car drive into his field and start toward them.

"Suddenly the car was not a car. Instead, it was two people coming at me with bright flashlights."

He said he had heard no one tell him he should stay where he was or that the persons with flashlights were wardens. He didn't know who they were, so he ran. He ran into the woods. After the struggle, in which the warden tried to shoot him, he was taken out of the woods.

Bert's story didn't hold much to the truth. It was hard for anyone to believe that, on such a quiet night, one couldn't distinguish a moving car from two walking men within 100 yards, much less the 50 feet Bert talked about. It was also hard to understand why a landowner would go into his fields to investigate some shooting and then run when he discovered people there—especially when the landowner was someone like Bert, with a reputation for violence.

The evidence that was to send him to the state penitentiary for one to seven years was something new to the courts of northern Wisconsin. The crime lab, using colored slides on a screen before the jury, showed how extractor marks (marks made by a gun's extractor when it ejects fired or unfired shells from a weapon), from shells found in Bert's house and shells he dropped on the ground, matched (like fingerprints) test shells ejected from the gun found in the woods.

It was hard to believe that Bert knew nothing about a gun that was tied indisputably to shells found in his house, on his bedroom dresser, and at his feet when he was about to be searched that night in the field. The gun was also tied to the two dead deer. Bullets proven to have been fired from that gun were found in both deer. The extractor marks on the unfired shells were there because Bert did what many hunters do when they hunt deer in the black of night. He fully loaded his gun to be ready to shoot as many times as might be necessary. Then, when circumstances caused no shots or few shots to be fired, the rest of the shells carried the extractor marks—"gun fingerprints"— that sent Bert Claud to the state penitentiary. Bert served only seven months of his one- to three-year sentence, but this was the first major trial conviction of a wildlife violator in that county in many years. Without the expert testimony by the crime lab witnesses, Bert would have gone free. Warden Kern went on to become a warden supervisor in southern Wisconsin. I went on, just a little bit wiser about how to handle violent nighttime deer hunters.

The ambush

I know I took chances when I contacted hunters and fishermen far back in the wilds of Wisconsin, Minnesota and New Hampshire; the rice fields of Arkansas; and the salt marshes of New York and Massachusetts. I made some careless moves but was fortunate: I came out alive. But when I think back to the biggest chance I took—the night of the ambush—I realize that it could have been my last mistake.

Joe Claud's car stood in the driveway, its motor still running. His wife was at the entryway to the darkened house. She appeared to be talking to someone—probably her husband—who stayed out of sight, just inside the doorway to his brother's house. We had pulled up just outside the driveway with our patrol car. There were four of us—two other wardens, undersheriff Norm Thompson, and myself.

We had come to serve a search warrant on the house of Joe Claud's brother. Bert Claud was in jail, charged with killing deer out of season and assaulting a conservation warden the night before. The two other wardens stationed themselves just outside the driveway, between the treeline. They were armed with high-powered rifles. The Claud brothers had a reputation for violence. Norm and I stood behind our patrol car, discussing what to do next.

Twenty minutes before, we had gone to Joe Claud's house just across the highway from his brother's. Norm and I had decided that even though we had a legal search warrant for Bert's house, we wanted someone from the family to be at the house when we searched. We wanted no false charges made against us later for theft of items from the house. Besides, it was just good business to have a family member there when we searched.

We were looking for evidence related to Bert's wholesale deer-slaughtering business and evidence of his deer killing of the night before. When we arrived at Joe's house, his wife and sixteen-year-old son came to the door. Norm and I read the warrant to them and asked if they would come over to Bert's house, to be there while we searched. Joe's wife told us her husband wasn't home and she wasn't about to go over to Bert's house.

"Is your husband over at Bert's house in the dark, waiting for someone, who might be coming to search it?" I asked. She wouldn't answer that question.

"If you wardens go over to that house, you'll come out in a different way than when you go in."

"We are going over there, and we are armed. If your husband is there, you better tell him we're coming. We will be serving and executing the search warrant in ten minutes."

We went out under the yard light in her driveway and proceeded to get out our weapons and prepare them so that she would, without question, get the message.

Two minutes later, before we could drive out of her yard, she and the boy raced out of the house, jumped into their car, and roared off toward Bert's house. We followed a few minutes later. Her car was there.

Norm and I decided we would approach the back door of the house, behind Joe's car, and try to talk Joe out of the house. We didn't want anyone to get hurt. This situation had all the ingredients for someone to catch a bullet.

Norm Thompson was a big, fearless professional. He knew what to say and what to do in an emergency. He wore a patch over one eye and could see better out of the one good eye than most of us could see out of two. That morning, he and I had returned to the fields just behind Bert Claud's house to look for evidence and make measurements in the area where the two deer were killed. In this area, Bert had assaulted one of the wardens who was attempting to arrest him.

"Get back here on the double!" Norm had suddenly shouted at me. I can still, in my mind, see Norm waving at me from his car. He had just driven into the field through the same fence opening we used the night before. I walked out toward where the deer had lain.

"All my tires are going flat. Someone has spiked the road," Norm said. I ran back, and we drove as fast as we could into town, getting to a service station just as all four Double Eagle whitewall tires went flat.

But now at Bert's house, we had problems more serious than flat tires. Someone could end up here flat on his back. The car with the sixteen-year-old was still running as Norm and I started up behind it. Norm called out toward the darkened doorway.

"Joe, if you are in there, come out, and keep your hands out where we can see them. There are two rifles trained on that doorway."

Norm and I were approaching with our sidearms still in their holsters. Joe's wife stood in the doorway. Suddenly she walked away and the young boy surprised us by driving the car, tires spinning, farther into the driveway. We were left exposed halfway to the door. I knew Norm and I were dead pigeons if Joe cut loose at us from the darkened doorway. We hit the ground and drew our weapons automatically.

"Come out, Joe, and don't do anything foolish," Norm said.

There was a shuffling inside the doorway, then a loud clunk, as if something had been set down in the corner. Then Joe appeared. His hands were empty and out where we could see them. Norm and I went

quickly to him. Just inside the doorway stood a shotgun in the corner.
It was loaded with double-aught buckshot. I knew from putting on gun-
safety demonstrations (shooting through engine blocks) what double-
aught buck would have done to Norm and me.

We searched the house and found the evidence we had described
in the warrant. I have always been thankful that we decided to give
the family the courtesy of being there when we searched Bert's dark
and "vacant" house.

Joe later told us he was prepared to shoot any "vandals" who
might come to steal from his brother's house while Bert was being held
"illegally" in jail. To this day I believe that had Joe's wife not gone
to him and told him how well armed we were and how many there
were of us, Joe would have shot the first "vandals" that approached
his brother's darkened doorway.

Wildlife officers to remember

There are hundreds of wildlife officers whom I have worked with
and will never forget. These officers had the same feelings about the
wildlife and the wilderness whether they wore a state or federal badge
or the badge of a Saskatchewan or British Columbian wildlife officer.
I can't name them all, but I will not forget what each one stood for in
his battle to protect the vulnerable wilderness and its wildlife.

There are several officers who guided and inspired me throughout
my thirty years of wildlife law-enforcement work—officers whose standards and accomplishments should remain examples to us all. Let me
tell you about these officers.

Ernie Swift not only cared about the wilderness, he did something
about it. Ernie believed with every fiber of his being that a person must
stand up for what he believes in. He believed in the protection of our
natural resources; and most important, he wasn't afraid to say so. Ernie
Swift began his long fight for the wilderness as a Wisconsin conservation warden. His now famous story of how he tangled with the
Chicago mobsters fishing illegally, when they retreated to northern
Wisconsin to get away from "kill or be killed," is history.

Arresting mobsters fishing below the Chippewa River dam illegally—when they packed a .45 on their hip and drove a car loaded
down with machine guns and sawed-off shotguns—did present com-
plications. But Ernie Swift handled them and survived. He went on to

become director of the Wisconsin Conservation Department (now called the Department of Natural Resources), and then assistant director of the U.S. Fish and Wildlife Service. He later became head of the National Wildlife Federation.

After Ernie retired, he wrote many articles for *National Wildlife* magazine. In his book, *Conservation Saga,* Ernie talked about "floating your own stick." He pointed out that it is most important to float one's own stick in life; but standing up for wilderness and wildlife, when it counts, is what conservation of our resources is all about.

I watched Ernie take on resort owners for unsafe boats, city fathers for locally polluted waters, industrialists for abusing the land and the lakes, and politicians for not seeming to care. When Ernie Swift died of a heart attack in 1968, he left behind an important message, one I will always cherish:

> If conservation is going to be effective, all citizens are going to have to feel a personal responsibility in regard to their own actions in relation to their use now and to future use of natural resources. People have to realize that something is wrong, and something has to be done about it.

Ernie and I used to sit for hours talking about the trials and joys and disappointments of our profession. We talked about the threats to our environment—pollution, litter, dumping, and dredging. We also talked about the general lack of understanding for wildlife law enforcement. When I think of someone who really was willing to float his own stick for the wilderness, I think of Ernie Swift.

George Hadland was the chief of the Wisconsin warden force when I first became a warden. He was one of the most dedicated conservationists I have ever known. George had the foresight that many of us lack in regard to our resources. He was criticized by many of his own officers for accepting more responsibilities, such as a boat safety program, for all his overworked and underpaid officers.

But George was proven right. He had great faith in many young, green conservation wardens. He gave them a chance to become professionals, and he did it with endless enthusiasm and respect. When I think of someone who cared and stood up for wildlife in his lifetime, I think of George Hadland. He retired in 1962, owing to failing health. George still bubbled with enthusiasm about the wilderness twenty years later, when I talked with him on the phone about wildlife and wildlife enforcement; it was an enthusiasm that burned perpetually within him. George died in March of 1982.

Agent Bill Kensinger and I banded ducks in Canada and chased waterfowl outlaws up and down the East coast. Bill and I were drawn together because we thought alike in regard to the rights and wrongs of resource management in this country. After about twenty-five years of wildlife enforcement work, we ended up as special agents-in-charge along the East coast; Bill was in Baltimore, I went to Boston.

Bill cared a great deal about his work. He was very good at what he did. I have always referred to him as a "deep-water man." When the going got tough, Bill always waded into the deepest water, the toughest place. Bill was a bright man and an extremely polished speaker; he carried his sincerity about wildlife protection from his toes to his eyes. The U.S. Fish and Wildlife Service lost more than an agent when Bill died of a heart attack in November, 1980, at an agent-in-charge conference in Virginia. We all lost a leader willing and able to float his own stick. Bill would have understood the words of this book. I know his wife Shirley will.

D. W. (Bill) Waggoner dedicated his whole life to the resource. You read about him in the early pages of this book. He was my first supervisor. Many of my early philosophies about the wilderness grew from seeds planted by Bill. He taught me that a good supervisor doesn't take away his subordinate's authority whenever it suits his fancy. Bill would step back and let us make our own way, right or wrong.

He was a muskie fisherman who often mentioned, with a sigh, the time he guided Gypsy Rose Lee on a muskie fishing trip. In later years, I converted Bill into a trout fisherman. Some of our best times together, besides the work we accomplished, were those infrequent days when we would head north to the Namekagon River with our fly rods, a frying pan, some cracker crumbs, a half-pound of butter, salt and pepper, a loaf of bread, and a six-pack of beer. The beer would cool in the river while we fished, and we would end the day on the banks of the river, watching the sun go down, with the smell of frying trout in the clear, cool air.

My biggest regret about Bill? I regret I lost my first boss and good friend to cancer before I had the chance to see him get back some of his share of the trout-fishing time he earned during his hard career. But I will always remember, as if it were yesterday, Bill coming up out of the trout stream, his old hat tilted back, his old brown shirt wet with sweat. When asked about his luck for the day, he would open his creel and ask, "Swen, where can you find a better life than this?"

I know of no one who worked harder or longer to protect the wildlife and wild places he loved so much. Bill seldom slept over five or six hours a night. To Bill Waggoner and his patient, loving wife, Gladys, my family and I owe more than we will ever be able to repay.

Big Ed Manthie taught me what honesty means in the tough occupation of a conservation warden. Always a gentleman, always straightforward, quiet, calm, and determined. Big Ed always had the right word for the good guy, and the right word for the bad. His wisest words ring true in my ears: "Be firm, but always be fair."

The name of Ed Manthie will long be respected in and around Ladysmith, Wisconsin, where he was stationed for many years. I had a few short moments to tell big Ed how I felt about our times together, and how important it was for me to spend my first training days with him. I talked to Ed and his wife in the hospital room by phone, one day several years ago. Both Ed and Rosemary were calm and sincerely thankful for my call that day. They also told me how thankful they were for their time together. Ed died of cancer the next day. I believe the Lord owes big Ed some fishing time too.

Little Ed Sealander has just retired as a warden supervisor at Park Falls in northern Wisconsin. I know little Ed's caring rubbed off on me. His endless patience and early guidance will never be forgotten. Little Ed honors me with an open invitation to stay at his cabin on the Flambeau River, an invitation Jackie and I have several times accepted. Now that Ed has recovered from open-heart surgery, we will meet again on the White, or the Longbranch or Ten Mile, to chase trout and talk about old times and the future of wild places and wild things. Maybe he can still imitate the loon on a quiet northern lake or the mountain lion we always heard but never saw. Ed Sealander will always remain my symbol of state wildlife officers who have dedicated their lives to the protection of wildlife and wildernesses everywhere.

My wilderness can survive

It was another Saturday morning in New England in 1984. Much had happened since Wisconsin's Spring Creek in 1954.

My dog Cassie and I were finally back to our early morning hike through the well kept cemetery and just beyond to "my" special piece of Massachusetts wilderness. I had been out of town on business for the last few weekends, and both the dog and I were eager to head for our pine knoll near the stream.

Then I heard a chainsaw. The sound was coming from the big pines where I was headed. I said to Cassie, "Maybe someone is cutting firewood just across the brook from my knoll." But in the back of my mind I knew there were few trees there, even for firewood.

As I puffed down the old horse trail, Cassie whipped by me, as she always did, going like the wind. Then I saw a Caterpillar tractor ahead through the pines, just beyond the 150-year-old stone wall that had guarded my wilderness since the local militia fought the British here in the 1700s.

I heard the chainsaw again, and heard the Cat purr as it moved toward me, belching smoke. Down crashed one of the big pines as the Cat put its bucket against the trunk and finished the job started by the chainsaw. I stood for a moment not wanting to believe what I saw; but before I could question what was happening, another large white pine came crashing down toward me. This one looked like it fell almost on top of my rocky knoll.

I walked up toward the noisy tractor and the buzzing saw. When I got to the knoll, I could look down through the tiny valley and see fallen giants in all directions. The fragrant smell of fresh cut pine was in the air. But the usual bird sounds were not to be heard above the din of man's machines.

I called the big yellow Lab that had replaced another. Before them there had been big old Midnight, the "black angus." He had lived to be almost fifteen years old and spent his last days chasing down big rooster pheasants in western Minnesota.

I remember his last hunt, when he chased a crippled cock across a plowed field. Old Mid's hind legs wouldn't do as they were told, so when all else failed, the big fading fighter dragged them behind to catch his last opponent. Midnight's career as a wildlife officer's helper had been a colorful one, highlighted by the night he stood guard over my seven *impressed* deer shiners.

Cassie and I now walked away from our usual rocky knoll, where a fallen giant now lay in the needles and decaying humus of the last centuries of change. Had I been younger and less seasoned as to this new change taking place this morning, I might have been as sad as I was that Saturday morning on Spring Creek in 1954. But my many years of working in the outdoors, attempting to protect wildlife and wild places had taught me that nothing is today as it was yesterday. I could see blue marks on the larger trees, which made me feel that this was going to be a selected cutting project. Maybe the owner of this little piece of wilderness would realize that he is only a temporary caretaker of this special place. Maybe this "landowner" would proceed cautiously as he intruded into this wilderness he called his own.

As I sat next to one of the fallen giants yet to be towed away by the Cat, I carefully counted the growth rings on its good-smelling stump. Cassie looked on as I smoothed her ears.

"This tree sprouted back in the early 1900s," I told her, "before World War I." It was just 70 years old. I examined the sap-filled growth rings of the last 30 years—my years carrying the badge of a wildlife officer. As in my career, there were good years of growth and progress and lean years when times were tough and nights were long. I looked down carefully at the rings and counted back to 1955. This tree was 43 years old in 1955, when I began my career in Wisconsin. Funny, this big, old white pine seemed to enjoy seven or eight good years of growth here in New England, while I was growing and learning and seasoning as a Wisconsin conservation warden, some 2,000 miles west of here. The old pine seemed to have some lean years about the time I left Wisconsin and began a new way of life as a federal agent in western Minnesota. Those were tough years for Jackie and me. We had two young children, and I was on the road chasing duck hunters much of the time all over the Midwest. Each summer I was sent to Canada for six weeks of banding waterfowl. If I were to check the weather bureau's records and compare them to the rings indicated, I would probably find conditions in Acton, Massachusetts weren't the best for white pine growth around 1963–65.

Cassie had found an appropriately sized stick and was saying, forget that tree stump, throw this stick for me to retrieve. She's a great retriever; in fact, I keep telling Jackie we should have named her One Track, because retrieving everything—from her duck dummy to balls and firewood from my neighbor's woodpile—was just about all she ever thought of. I always told the mailman, "If I could throw you over the stone wall next to the house, Cassie would bring you back too."

But ignoring the dog and her pleading eyes and the Cat and the buzzing of the chainsaw, I concentrated again on the pine stump. Nineteen sixty-nine was a good white pine year in back of the cemetery. That was also the year we moved to New England and fell in love with the ocean, the mountains, and the old stone walls. And I also learned, in those early seventies when the pine was doing pretty well, that New England and the East coast had environmental problems too.

I think it was 1971 when the New Hampshire Fish and Game Department, the Society for the Protection of New Hampshire's Forests, the local newspapers, and many other people besides myself, went to war to stop a Massachusetts outfit from dredging the bottom of beautiful Lake Umbagog for diatomaceous earth to be used for filtering swimming pools.

The lake lies on the Maine–New Hampshire border and to this day does not harbor any dredging barges or have any processing plants intruding on its secluded, wildlife-filled shores. But that battle is renewed every few years. Spoilers, calling themselves "soldiers of progress," don't give up; they just reassemble to find another way to get what they think they must have and can get from the "endless" resources of this nation.

I had thought about Spring Creek, and the many lost ones like it, when we were fighting for Umbagog's survival. I also remembered Ernie Swift and his thoughts about "floating your own stick." I think people like Ernie Swift, Bill Waggoner, George Hadland, and Big and Little Ed, had convinced me that a person must stand up for what he says he believes in. I guess that's the one quality I found so prevalent in wildlife officers and that I admired more than any other.

I know I haven't agreed with all the officers I have known and worked with, but I sure knew where they stood. They were, almost without exception, ready to stand up and be counted—even when it would have been easier to drift into the edge of the woods and remain silent.

The old pine seemed to recognize 1980 as a year when environmental issues and pine trees were not at the top of the priority list of this nation's leaders. The old pine's growth ring in '80 was hard to find. I'm sure its inhibited growth was physical, rather than mental. I'm sure the pine, hidden back here in the secluded woods behind the cemetery, hadn't heard the name James Watt. But then again, I do talk out loud to the dog back here on Saturday mornings.

Cassie and I head home. We've decided our woods will be okay. We are betting on the owner to take out the harvestable timber and leave the rest to the horses. Wildernesses survive in strange ways and for strange reasons: as cemetery grounds, because of eccentric little old ladies, or even because of an understanding public. But in this case I think it was horses.

Very early Sunday morning, Cassie and I went back to the pine knoll to check on the "progress" the Cat had made. We found our rock still there. Many fallen giants had been towed away. Chainsaws and Caterpillar tractors don't usually work on Sundays and this Sunday they observed that tradition.

The crows and bluejays and nuthatches serenaded. A mallard set her wings over my head and glided into the brook. Then her mate, with his bright green plumage, splashed in alongside her, cackling. I could hear the cars on the road across the brook. People roared by, not knowing about this little piece of wilderness just across the brook from their hectic life. My pine knoll has changed, but survived.

There have been many changes in our nation's wildlife and wildernesses. During the thirty years, we have caused species of wildlife to become extinct and others to become endangered. I have watched as mountains disappeared, pristine rivers were dammed, and wildlife and its habitat were sold down the river by people who said they were "making wise use of the resources." James Watt's land-use philosophies will haunt our children's children long after Watt and I have turned to dust.

But almost every day that I traveled in the nation's outdoors, I met more people who cared about wild places and wild creatures. Many didn't even know why wild things were important, but at least they recognized that importance. New organizations, concerned about pollution, seals, whales, turtles, and redwoods, have sprung up. They are made up of ordinary people, not just people who have studied and worked and dedicated their lives to the outdoors. They have begun to worry about a country that could become so concerned about the gross national product that our umbilical ties to the land would be forgotten. I have seen many of these caring people get involved, not always doing the right thing, but getting involved and "floating their own stick" for what they believe in.

There will always be violators of the fish and game laws. I have learned to live with that. But there will also be caring people who know down deep that they must be responsible for their acts against nature. Wildlife regulations and wildlife officers are an integral and inseparable management tool that holds people to their responsibilities in the outdoors. Without enforcement, laws and regulations soon become a mockery. And I believe that without wildlife officers, there would be no wilderness places—and before long no wildlife.

In his book, *Conservation Saga,* Ernie Swift spoke of children and what they might inherit from us:

> Teach your child that freedom and liberty will survive only in proportion to the responsibility and restraint that are exercised. Teach him to create a culture of which he will be the beneficiary and not the victim.
>
> Teach him that a sunset over a verdant countryside has more intrinsic value than the most costly painting; that outdoor recreation should not be peddled on the street corners; and that wildlife should not be weighed and sold by the pound. Teach him that bread comes from the soil and not from the store; teach him that fat cities do not thrive on lean countrysides.
>
> We will be judged by our offspring, and in that judgement if all they can contemplate is muddy and polluted rivers, eroded hillsides, burned forest lands, and wildlife behind glass, stuffed, then they will have a right to ponder just what type of improvident barbarians sired them.

In museum area of Perkins School for the Blind, Watertown (Boston), Massachusetts, students can handle mounted specimens of birds of prey and other creatures, the better to "visualize" the size and texture of wildlife. Swendsen and his staff got involved in furnishing such specimens. *Photo by Bill Whalen, U.S. Fish and Wildlife Service*

In *Sand County Almanac,* Aldo Leopold wrote, "When we see the land as a community to which we belong, we may begin to use it with love and respect."

A land without wilderness places and wild living things? Rachel Carson warned us in her *Silent Spring:* "There was no sound; only the silence lay over the woods and marsh." Instead of permitting this frightening silence, man can choose to be the difference. People are just people; but within the hands of the people portrayed in this book, and others like them, lies the future of America's wildlife and wilderness places. After thirty years of carrying a badge in the wilderness, I feel confident that man does care, that he will stand tall and "float his own stick" to see that there will be an America tomorrow—a tomorrow filled with the mystical sounds and wondrous sights of nature. And it probably won't surprise you to know I am still fascinated by the antics of wild animals, the smell of a pine tree, and the wonder and unpredictability of the human species.